Page

ACRONYMS

GWOT	Global War on Terrorism
HAMAS	Harakat al-Muqawama or Islamic Resistance Movement
PLO	Palestinian Liberation Organization
US	United States

ILLUSTRATIONS

TABLES

CHAPTER 1

INTRODUCTION

America is the number one enemy of the deprived and oppressed people of the world. There is no crime America will not commit in order to maintain its political, economical, cultural, and military domination of those parts of the world where it predominates. It exploits the oppressed people of the world by means of the large-scale propaganda campaigns that are coordinated for it by international Zionism. By means of its hidden and treacherous agents, it sucks the blood of the defenseless people as if it alone, together with its satellites, had the right to live in this world (Makdisi 2002, 551).
Ruhollah Khomeini, Islam and Revolution

Introduction

As the above quote indicates, there is a prevalence of anti-Americanism in the world, especially in the Middle East. This thesis investigates the root causes of the anti-American phenomenon throughout the Arab Muslim Middle East. Particularly, the thesis question is: Is Arab Muslim antipathy in the Middle East toward the United States (US) based on US policies in the region, specifically relating to the Israeli and Palestinian conflict?

This thesis utilizes quantitative survey data to investigate the degree of anti-American sentiment among Arab Muslims while using various sources to reveal the qualitative views that support this data. This thesis will examine the data to determine if Arab Muslim anti-Americanism is primarily precipitated by America's actions. That is, do Arab Muslims dislike the US because of its actions in the region and around the world relating specifically to US policies in support of Israel?

Arab Muslim anti-Americanism is a very complex phenomenon and thus is very difficult to understand. Therefore, this thesis will also investigate and analyze two additional contributing factors termed clashing cultures and self-interested manipulation by Middle Eastern governments or influential Arab groups. These contributing factors, in conjunction with US polices, may determine the extent of Arab Muslim anti-American sentiment. Finally, this thesis will outline some suggestions for dealing with this growing anti-American phenomenon and will show how this anti-American sentiment is hindering US efforts in the Global War on Terrorism (GWOT) or otherwise known as the Long War.

Background

Arab Muslim anti-Americanism is a much younger phenomenon than its European counterpart. Although it shares many similarities with European anti-Americanism, Arab Muslim anti-Americanism only became widespread after the US' open support for Israel after the 1967 Six Day War. In fact, several years earlier, Arab Muslims had been supportive of the US because of the US' support to Egypt's Nasser regime. However, since 1967 the US has been considered by many Arab Muslims incomprehensibly pro-Israeli.

Anti-American feelings among Arab Muslims in the Middle East are extremely high and this resentment appears to be on the rise. On the surface, the reasons behind these anti-American feelings are more difficult to explain than they may seem. The phenomenon behind these feelings is far more varied and complex than can be conveyed by the images of protesters in a variety of Middle Eastern countries who demand the end of US aggression or condemn Israel. The image of the US to many in the Middle East is low and US policies in the region appear to be making this image worse.

What is the US' image in the Middle East? Is anti-Americanism really on the rise in the Middle East? Is there blind hatred of the US among Arab Muslims? These questions and others are vitally important and must be investigated and analyzed in order to determine the causes of this ever increasing trend.

Problem Statement

The Middle East region has significant strategic importance to the US because the region provides more than 20 percent of the US' total oil imports each year. The Middle East region is also important to the world's economy because it boasts a rich endowment of natural resources--including approximately two-thirds of the world's known oil reserves--a large labor force and a respected tradition of trade.

Currently, the US is engaged militarily in several countries within the Middle East as part of its efforts in the GWOT. Due to these engagements, a majority of Arab Muslims in the Middle East deeply resent the US and consequently are hindering US efforts in the region. The GWOT is not only a war between fighting forces but also a war between competing ideas. That is, in order to be successful in the GWOT, the US must not only win military battles but must also win the battle of ideas. Specifically, the US must earn the support of the Arab Muslim population, and in order to earn this support the US must reverse the Arab Muslim feeling of resentment toward the US.

There is no single, agreed upon reason for Arab Muslim anti-Americanism. However, there are a variety of views that attempt to explain the cause of anti-American resentment. For instance, some scholars, such as Harvard Professor Samuel Huntington, argue the Arab Muslim anti-Americanism is a result of clashing cultures (1996, 101) while others, such as the Director of the Global Research in International Affairs, Barry

Rubin, argue this anti-American sentiment is simply a product of self-interested manipulation by Middle Eastern governments or various influential groups within the Arab society (2004, 81). Additionally, others such as Professor Juan Cole, argue that Arab Muslim anti-Americanism is a result of the US policy in the Middle East, specifically the perceived unbalanced support the US gives to Israel in terms of the Israeli and Palestinian conflict (2006, 1129). Regardless, Arab Muslim resentment is increasing and has caused regional instability; it has hampered US efforts in the GWOT, and has resulted in an ever increasing threat to US interests around the world. Therefore, in order to be successful in the region the US must attempt to reduce this resentment. If the US does not attempt to reduce Arab Muslim resentment, regional instability will likely continue to increase, US progress in the GWOT in the region will likely continue to slow, and US interests will likely remain a target.

Arab Muslim Resentment Toward the United States

Among the majority of Arab Muslims, the expression of anti-American sentiment stems less from a blind hatred of the US than from a profound ambivalence about the US. The US was once an object of admiration for many within the Arab community because of its affluence and technology. However, now the US is a source of deep disappointment given the perceived ongoing role of the US in shaping a repressive Middle Eastern status quo. Anti-Americanism is not a consistent ideology. That is, its intensity, coherence and evidence vary across the Arab world. Yet, it is important to understand the level, nature, and origins of this ever growing anti-American sentiment (Makdisi 2002, 539).

Level of Resentment

Rarely has the US had consistent stable relations with many Middle Eastern countries. However, since the US led GWOT began in 2001 relations have seriously deteriorated, resulting in an increasingly unfavorable opinion of the US in a majority of countries in the region. But how bad is it?

Various organizations have conducted world opinion surveys throughout the world to identify trends among various demographic groups as well as to determine people's attitudes, beliefs, and desires. Survey data compiled after 11 September 2001, demonstrate there is indeed a growing anti-American trend among Arab Muslims.

According to an article in the 23 July 2004, edition of the *Washington Post*, survey data from 2004 clearly showed that anti-American sentiment among Arab Muslims was high and rising. Specifically, a 2002 Zogby International survey showed 76 percent of Egyptians had a negative attitude toward the US, which increased to 98 percent in 2004. Additionally, in Saudi Arabia, such responses rose from 87 percent in 2002 to 94 percent in 2004 (Linzer 2004, A26).

Polling data from 2005 and 2006 showed little difference from previous surveys. For example, in six "friendly" Middle Eastern countries, only 12 percent of those surveyed expressed favorable attitudes toward the US. This survey also showed that US leaders had surpassed Israeli leaders as a major object of Arab anger (Regan 2007, 99).

More recently, a survey conducted by the University of Maryland in conjunction with Zogby International found that 78 percent of Arabs had an unfavorable view of the US. Additionally, this survey showed that 72 percent of Arabs see the US as the biggest "state threat" (Syed 2007).

Finally, another world opinion survey conducted by Gallup's Center for Muslim Studies revealed that 52 percent of Iranians have an unfavorable view of the US. However, surprisingly the antipathy toward the US in Iran is lower than the antipathy in other countries like Saudi Arabia and Jordan--all supposedly close allies of the US. In fact, over two-thirds of Jordanians and Pakistanis, and a staggering 79 percent of Saudis, have a negative view of their friend and ally (Syed 2007).

Origin of Resentment

This thesis investigates the origins of the anti-American phenomenon in the Arab Middle East to determine if it is based on US policies in the Middle East, specifically the US policy as it relates to Israel. Anti-Americanism cannot be explained simply by investigating US policies, because anti-Americanism is extremely complex. Therefore, in order to understand Arab Muslim anti-Americanism this thesis will investigate other contributing factors of this phenomenon and analyze them to determine how these factors are inter-related to US policies and to each other.

US regional policies and support for Israel. Due to the region's strategic importance and vitally important resources, many US leaders have pursued and engaged in a very aggressive foreign policy in the Middle East region. It is this aggressive foreign policy, especially in Iraq, the GWOT and Israel that recent world opinion data shows is the main cause of Arab Muslim resentment toward the US. Also, according to world opinion data, it is commonly believed among Arab Muslims that the US is not involved in the region to promote democracy or free the oppressed but rather to gain control of the region's oil supplies, support Israel, or achieve world domination. Thus anti-

Americanism is characterized by an identification of American power as a force for repression, rather than liberation of Arab Muslims.

In regards to US policy in the region, most anti-American feelings are clearly rooted in the fact that the US is siding strongly with one party, Israel, in the ongoing Israeli and Palestinian conflict. It is this issue, and this issue alone, that this thesis will investigate as the basis for Arab Muslim resentment of the US.

If the US policy in support of Israel is the basis of anti-American sentiment, then what exactly is the policy? How long has the US been supporting Israel and why is this support so important to the Arab Muslim population?

After World War II, the US gradually replaced France and Britain as the major power in the Middle East. Fair or not, many Arab Muslims transferred their grievances toward and distrust of Paris and London to Washington. Initially, the US showed sympathy for local nationalist aspirations and urged the end of colonialism. However, US motives were not necessarily in line with many Middle Eastern countries. US interventionism was driven by anticommunism, not Arab nationalism (Cole 2006, 1127).

During the 1950s and 1960s, regional conflicts and Cold War alliances shaped Middle Eastern attitudes toward the US. As the US allied more and more strongly with Israel, Arab regimes began to seek other external support. For instance, nations such as Egypt, Syria, Libya, Yemen, and Iraq all developed close ties with the Soviet Union, and thus regimes and their publics came to be critical of the US (Cole 2006, 1127).

The Arab-Israeli conflict increasingly polarized the region, especially in 1967, when the Arabs were embarrassed during the Six-Day War, and Israel occupied Jerusalem and thereafter governed over the stateless Palestinians of the West Bank and

Gaza. As Israel started to expand their power throughout a variety of territories, they evoked shock and outrage from the Arab Muslim community. It eventually became evident that the US would do nothing to stop this Israeli expansion; therefore, the US earned a share of the hostility directed by Arabs Muslims toward Israel (Cole 2006, 1127).

The US continued support for Israel during the Arab-Israeli War of 1973 is another example of how the US policy in the region favored Israel. As a result of US support for Israel during this period, many oil producing nations in the region emplaced an embargo against the US. Additionally, this war signaled an increased commitment by the US to negotiate and guarantee Arab-Israeli agreements, but above all else it demonstrated how the US would continue to support Israel.

Throughout the next two decades, the US policy in the region would be based on continued support of Israel, in the form of diplomatic, military, and economic aid. This was especially the case during the 1987 Intifada, where the US vetoed several pro-Palestinian United Nations Security Council Resolutions in support of Israel.

Most recently, the US' unconditional support for Israel while Israel launched two wars has added to the unfavorable image of the US in the Middle East. This most recent support for Israel and the US' failure to respect the democratic choice of Palestinians has turned organizations like HAMAS (Harakat al-Muqawama or Islamic Resistance Movement) and Hezbollah (Party of God) into symbols of resistance and thus reduced the chance for the US to improve its image in the region.

Contributing Factors

Arab Muslim anti-Americanism can not be investigated and analyzed solely in terms of what the US does (US policies) but it must also be viewed in conjunction with other contributing factors. The two main contributing factors, combined with US policies, which cause the complex anti-American phenomenon, are what can be termed as clashing cultures and self interested manipulation by Middle Eastern governments or influential Arab groups.

1. Clashing cultures. To understand this anti-American antipathy in the Middle East one must first understand what can be termed the Arab Muslim civilization. Specifically, one must understand what drives Arab Muslim attitudes, motivations, and feelings. Once one understands the Arab Muslim civilization one may gain an understanding of why so many Arab Muslims have a negative view of the US.

Many Arab Muslims are convinced that the US, and perhaps the West, is their enemy. According to world opinion surveys, Arab Muslims are becoming less nationalistic and more Islamic. That is, they do not see themselves first as a Jordanian or Saudi Arabian but rather as Muslims. The Arab Muslim civilization is growing beyond national borders and thus uniting groups of individuals not formerly united. As a result, anti-American, Islamic movements around the Arab Muslim world are uniting under a common bond of feeling oppressed at the hands of the US.

2. Self-interested manipulation by Middle Eastern governments or influential Arab groups. For years now, anti-Americanism has served as a means by which failed political systems and other types of movements in the Middle East tried to improve their overall standing within the Arab community. The US is blamed for what is bad in the

9

Arab world and is used as an excuse for political and social oppression and economic stagnation. By assigning responsibility for their own shortcomings to the US, Arab political, social, and religious leaders have distracted their populations' attention from the internal struggles that are their real problems. Thus rather than pushing for greater privatization, equality for women, democracy, civil society, freedom of speech, due process of law, or similar developments; the public focuses instead on hating the US (Rubin 2004, 73).

Similarly, Arab Muslims are increasingly aware that they have suffered one-half a century of defeats despite their attempts at militancy and mobilization. The material and technological gap between themselves and the West is widening, and Arab Muslims seem unable to get rid of authoritative regimes. Rulers who want to remain in power, intellectuals who foster different ideologies and clerics fearful of secularist trends find it easy and beneficial to blame the US for all their shortcomings and problems. The causes of all their problems are not their own power, the deficient systems and bad choices they make, but rather US intervention in the region (Rubin 2004, 22-23).

Definitions

Throughout this thesis, generalities will be used when defining certain groups or regions. The writer recognizes from the outset the limits of generalizing. Nevertheless, in order to investigate the recent rise in anti-Americanism among Arab Muslims in terms of the primary origin and contributing factors people and areas must be grouped together generally.

1. Anti-Americanism. In order to truly examine Arab Muslim antipathy toward the US, anti-Americanism must first be defined. Anti-Americanism is not defined as

hatred for individual Americans, nor necessarily the US culture. If fact, many Arab Muslims respect Americans because of their hard work ethic, freedoms, and desire to improve themselves. Therefore, anti-Americanism is really a hatred not of Americans themselves but of what America is understood to stand for. That is, what America is understood to be as a symbolic representation (Breyfogle 2004, 260).

2. Arab Muslims. The term Arab Muslims has already been used throughout this introductory chapter, however, it is important to understand how this writer determines what defines the Arab Muslim ethnic group. The Arab world spans over two continents, consists of 23 countries and has approximately 325 million people. Each of these countries has their own tradition and history and thus to properly represent this world demographic the scope of what is considered an Arab Muslim for this thesis must be narrowed. In terms of this thesis, Arab Muslims are considered to be Muslims from the Asian or Middle Eastern Arab World, which is comprised of the Arabian Peninsula, and Bilad al-Sham or the Levant. Specifically, the Arabian Peninsula is defined as the countries of: Bahrain, Iraq, Jordan, Kuwait, Oman, Qatar, Saudi Arabia, United Arab Emirates, and Yemen. Additionally, the Bilad al-Sham is the name for the whole Levant or "Greater Syria" region that today contains Syria, Jordan, Lebanon, Israel, and the Palestinian territory (Nevo and Pappe 1994, 95). Finally, due to its proximity and its influence throughout the region, the population of Egypt in the term Arab Muslims has also been included.

Additionally, there are two major Islamic sects: Sunni and Shiite. The two sects are similar, although the Shiites exalt their Imams as a line of inspired teachers. The split between the sects stems from the early days of Islam and arguments over Mohammed's successors as caliph or leader. Generally, the Sunni population comprises approximately 85 to 90 percent of all Muslims. The majority of Muslim nations are Sunni. Iran is the only nation with an overwhelmingly Shiite population; however, Iraq, Bahrain, and Lebanon do have large Shiite populations. For this thesis, when using the term Arab Muslims the Sunni population will only be considered within the Arab world previously defined.

3. Arab Muslim Civilization. In defining the term Arab Muslim civilization, this writer is focusing largely on what Samuel Huntington describes in his book titled *The Clash of Civilizations and the Remaking of World Order*. In a sense, the Arab Muslim civilization is the notion of being Muslim before being something else. According to Huntington, civilizations share common blood, language, and a way of life but most importantly a civilization is defined by a common religion (Huntington 1996, 47). Therefore, the Arab Muslim civilization is composed of a majority of Arab Muslims who identify themselves first as Muslims and secondly as Jordanians, Saudis, or Egyptians. It is the belief that Islam, with all its practices, cultures, and beliefs comes before nationalism. All Arab Muslims are united together; they are members of one larger Arab Muslim civilization. To them, national borders are only lines drawn on a map, temporarily limiting the Arab Muslim civilization from uniting.

The term Arab Muslim civilization is similar to the term Pan-Arabism in that both unite groups of a similar culture. However, the Arab Muslim civilization is slightly different from Pan-Arabism because unlike Pan-Arabism it is not secular or nationalistic. Pan-Arabism is often defined as a movement for unification of Arab peoples and nations of the Middle East based on the common Arab culture. Pan-Arabism is a form of cultural nationalism. The two terms are different because Pan-Arabism is linked to nationalism within the Arab world and the Arab Muslim Civilization is linked mainly by what Huntington argues as the single most defining characteristic of a civilization, religion (1996, 47). Thus, the Arab Muslim Civilization is a distinct sub-civilization within the larger world Islamic civilization.

Limitations

In conducting this thesis, survey data will be utilized to investigate the extent of Arab Muslims antipathy toward the US. However, it is neither feasible nor desirable to conduct new surveys in order to investigate the level of antipathy within the Arab Muslim world. Therefore, this study will draw on previously conducted surveys and is subject to each survey's specific questions, locations, and computations. This thesis will utilize and interpret this data but can not affect how or where the data was collected.

Delimitations

Arab Muslim resentment toward the US is not a new phenomenon. However, this thesis can not examine the entire history of these anti-American feelings. The focus will be on the more recent anti-American antipathy within the Arab Muslim population. Consequently, survey data prior to September 2001 will not be used.

Additionally, the US policy as it relates to the Israeli and Palestinian conflict is very complex. This thesis can not attempt to investigate and analyze each facet of this policy. Therefore, this thesis will only generalize and summarize the policy and its affects in the region. Specifically, this thesis will examine US policy and its affects during major incidents since the 1967 Six-Day War.

Significance of the Study

The United States is currently engaged in what can potentially be a very long and costly war against terror. The majority of this war must be fought in the Middle East and must be fought in conjunction with nations from the Middle East. Additionally, this war can not be only a military fight but the US must also fight the war of ideas. In order to win the war of ideas, the US must begin to reduce the idea of anti-Americanism and gain the support of the Arab Muslim world. It is imperative that the US gain assistance from not only the governments, but more importantly, the people within the Middle East. Without the assistance from Arab Muslims, the US will not be successful in the Long War. Therefore, the US must do what it can to gain the support of the Arab Muslims.

Why is this important to military personnel? It is important because for many Arab Muslims the only interaction they have with Americans is with US military personnel. For that reason, military personnel must understand that what they do and how they act is a direct reflection of what Arab Muslims think of Americans. Military personnel, especially leaders, are not only on the front lines of military actions in the Middle East but also on the front lines in terms of the war of ideas. And if the US wants to win the war of ideas, military personnel must understand and respect the Arab Muslim population, act accordingly and engage in constructive dialogue with the population to ensure a successful battle of ideas in the Long War.

In the next chapter, the published works concerning US policy in regards to the Israeli and Palestinian conflict and the Arab Muslim culture will be reviewed. Additionally, the arguments set forth by many attempting to explain Arab Muslim anti-American sentiment will be reviewed.

CHAPTER 2

LITERATURE REVIEW

Introduction

Many have researched and written about the phenomena of Arab Muslim anti-American sentiment in an effort to understand the causes, examine its effects, and attempt to identify potential courses of action to reverse this increasing trend. As a result, numerous articles, journals, speeches, and books on the topic have been published. The purpose of this chapter is to review literature on Arab Muslim antipathy toward the US in relating to this thesis. The compilation of various resources drawn upon for this thesis can be classified into three categories:

1. US regional policies and support for Israel

2. Clashing cultures

3. Self-interested manipulation by Middle Eastern governments or influential Arab groups

This review will follow the three aforementioned categories. However, several additional resources used in this thesis can be included in more than one of the three referenced categories because the authors provide evidence for the Arab Muslim anti-American sentiment in more than one of these three categories. Additionally, several resources were used that did not discuss Arab Muslim anti-American sentiment but did provide further insight into the Arab Muslim culture and the Israeli and Palestinian conflict. In cases such as these, the resource will be reviewed in the category which follows most closely to the authors' main argument or subject matter. Finally, this review will not cover the numerous periodical sources whose contribution to this thesis is limited

15

to providing only background information or confirmation of anti-American sentiment found in other source.

United States Regional Policies and Support for Israel

This thesis focuses on how the US Middle Eastern policies, specifically US support for Israel, affect Arab Muslim antipathy toward the US. This review will begin with literature that examines the Israeli and Palestinian conflict as well as literature that contends that, US actions in the region (policies) are the primary cause for Arab Muslim anti-American resentment.

An outstanding source that provided an enormous amount of information on the history of and current status of the Israeli and Palestinian conflict was the book titled *War without End: Israelis, Palestinians, and the Struggle for a Promised Land* written by Anton La Guardia. This book described in detail the nature of Israel and Palestine, the symbolism they represent, the mirror histories of their people, and the extraordinary power that this tiny country exerts across the globe (La Guardia 2003, xix).

In his book, La Guardia examines the ongoing struggle between the Israelis and Palestinians from both points of view. That is, throughout the book he does not argue the facts but rather provides the facts and shows how each side of this conflict and their supporters interprets these facts. La Guardia clearly demonstrates how this land is a land of two people whose lives are intertwined.

This book begins by providing an in-depth history of the land. That is, La Guardia explains why historically this land is so important to both Jews and Muslims. He continues to explain the formation of the current nation of Israel and then provides the historical facts behind Israel's survival as an independent nation within the region.

The majority of the book focuses on the history of this heavily contested region within the Middle East. La Guardia details the various conflicts in 1948, 1956, 1967, 1973, the Palestinian Intifada, and the second Palestinian Intifada of 2000. While analyzing these conflicts, La Guardia examines how and why they were fought and, more importantly, how the results of these conflicts have affected the feelings and attitudes of the participants and supporters, on both sides, and, as well as, governmental policies within the region.

Finally, La Guardia reviews the history of US support for Israel. La Guardia examines this support that has continued since President Truman recognized Israel as the de facto authority in the territory in May 1948. La Guardia concludes by demonstrating how US support of Israel has increased resentment of the US by many Arab Muslims.

A journal article that discusses anti-Americanism in regards to US policy was written by Professor Juan Cole. Dr. Cole's article published in the October 2006 *American Historical Review* titled "AHR Forum: Anti-Americanism: It's the Policies" briefly reviews and analyzes anti-Americanism in Latin America, Europe, and Asia. After reviewing anti-Americanism in these regions, Dr. Cole examines anti-Americanism in the Middle East in order to determine if the generalizations of anti-Americanism from the other regions of the world apply to the Middle East.

In examining anti-Americanism in the Middle East, Dr. Cole argues that Arab Muslim anti-American sentiment is rooted in US foreign policy, specifically, the US' policy in support of Israel and, even more now, the perceived brutal occupation of Iraq. Dr. Cole does not believe that Arab Muslim anti-American sentiment is a result of clashing cultures but rather shows recent polling data that demonstrates how this sentiment is based on US policies.

In August 2005, the editors of the periodical *The Nation* published an article titled "Unintended Consequences: A Forum on Iraq and the Mideast." This article is a composition of a series of questions and the answers the editors asked to four leading experts in the Middle East. Theses experts were asked to give their assessment of the consequences of the Bush Administration's policies in the region and America's standing within it. The four experts were: Helena Cobban, who writes the weblog JustWorldNews and is a columnist for the Christian Science Monitor and Al-Hayat (London); Juan Cole, a professor of history at the University of Michigan, who writes the weblog Informed Comment; Nir Rosen, a fellow at the New America Foundation and a reporter and author, who wrote a book titled *In the Belly of the Green Bird: The Triumph of the Martyrs in Iraq*; and Shibley Telhami, Anwar Sadat Professor for Peace and Development at the University of Maryland.

The article mainly focuses on US policy in terms of Iraq and how the policy has increased anti-Americanism among Arab Muslims. In this article all of the experts agree that it is the US policy in the Arab Muslim world that is the basis for anti-American sentiment. However, the article does suggest that US polices in the region have ignited an Islamic response and provides some evidence in support of the clash of civilizations theory.

Another useful source in regards to US policies in the region was Hubert Vedrine's article "On Anti-Americanism" published in the winter/spring 2004 *Brown Journal of World Affairs* which provides an interesting perspective on Arab Muslim anti-

American sentiment. The article does not solely focus on Arab Muslim anti-Americanism but also examines European and Latin American anti-Americanism. In terms of Arab Muslim anti-American sentiment, Vedrine argues that US support for Israel in the region is the sole cause of the phenomenon and if the US could bring about a fair solution to the Israeli and Palestinian crisis, Arab Muslim anti-American sentiment would drastically be reduced.

Additionally, another very helpful article examining Arab Muslim antipathy toward the US was an article written by Ussama Makdisi, an Associate Professor in the Department of History at Rice University. Dr. Makdisi's article in the *Journal of American History* titled "Anti-Americanism' in the Arab World: An Interpretation of a Brief History" reviews the rise of Arab Muslim anti-American sentiment over the past two centuries. Dr. Makdisi argues that Arab Muslim anti-Americanism is not a clash of civilizations but rather is a result of modern politics. Dr. Makdisi further argues that the US, once admired in the region, has been transformed into a figure of hostility due to its policies in support of Israel.

The final source in regards to US policies in the region was Abdallah Battah's article "Proximate and Permissive Causes of Anti-Americanism in the Arab Middle East." This article argues anti-Americanism can only be understood as a complex, multilayered phenomenon. Battah argues that there are four proximate causes (layers) of Arab Muslim anti-Americanism. These four causes are what he terms as: (1) US policies, its pronounced vision for the region and the American media; (2) pan-Arabists and radical Islamists who reject the colonial breakup of the region into a multitude of "nominally independent states" and aspire to create instead Arab or Islamic unity; (3)

manipulative regimes engaged in scapegoating or appeasing domestic forces; and (4) revolutionaries who wish to topple pro-Western regimes (Battah 2006). Battah further argues that these causes of anti-Americanism are complimentary and overlap but anti-Americanism forms and is permitted to grow because the weak and permissive Arab state and system.

Battah concludes this article by proposing some recommendations to reduce Arab Muslim anti-American sentiment. These recommendations range from pursing policies that promote US interest without undermining the interest of the people in the region to reassessing the US position on dealing with Islamic groups.

Clashing Cultures

Another cause, espoused by many, believe Arab Muslim antipathy toward the US is not based on what the US does but rather is a result of two separate clashing cultures. That is, the Arab Muslim culture, specifically the Islamic religion, clashes with the US democratic, free market belief system. Some authors, whose works are reviewed here, believe that the Arab Muslim culture is incompatible with the US culture and thus has caused anti-Americanism to rise in the region.

It is best to begin this section of literature review by discussing *The Clash of Civilizations and the Remaking of World Order*. This book was written by Harvard Professor Samuel P. Huntington, and many consider it one of the most influential pieces of literature that argues that the differences between the West and the rest of the world is based on a clash of cultures. In his book, Dr. Huntington argues that the world has undergone a paradigm shift in terms of international politics caused by the end of the Cold War. Dr. Huntington argues that because the Cold War has ended, the world will no longer be split between two superpowers with opposing ideologies and thus, future conflicts will not be based on opposing political ideologies. Rather, Dr. Huntington argues that the source of future international tension and conflicts will be based on opposing civilizations or cultures. Simultaneously, cultures will engage in cooperation with countries or groups which share a common culture (1996, 126). He further states that the conflicts of global politics will occur between nations and groups of different civilizations. It will be this clash that will dominate international politics and will be the battle lines of the future.

Dr. Huntington defines a civilization as a cultural entity and is thus the broadest level of cultural identity by which someone distinguishes themselves. Dr. Huntington states that a civilization is defined by a common objective, language, history, custom but most importantly a common religion (1996, 47). He goes further to state that because of the recent revitalization of cultural identities throughout the world, civilizations will become more important in the future.

Dr. Huntington gives numerous examples to defend his argument; however, he focuses mainly on the Balkan region and the conflict between the Orthodox Serbs, Catholic Croatians, and Bosnian Muslims. He uses this conflict to demonstrate how battle lines were drawn strictly between cultures. Dr. Huntington also uses this conflict to show how influential nations throughout the international community, with the exception of the US, supported the group of people most similar to itself in culture and how these three groups became more and more extreme in the belief of "us" versus "them" in terms of cultural identities (1996, 266). He argues that this kind of conflict will become the trend of the future, as more and more people begin to see a world in terms of one culture versus another culture.

Finally, Dr. Huntington argues that the main conflict in the future will be between Western culture and Islamic culture. He believes this for several reasons. One reason is because of the way the Western culture has dominated the globe politically, economically, and militarily over the last several decades. Secondly, he argues that both the Western and Islamic cultures feel they should be the dominant culture of the world. Finally, he argues that the greatest resistance to the western global domination has come from Islam because of its cultural assertiveness embodied in the Islamic Resurgence (1996, 209-218).

A tremendous resource for this thesis, providing an insight into Islam, was the book titled, *The Crisis of Islam: Holy War and Unholy Terror* written by renowned Middle East expert Bernard Lewis. In the first few chapters, Lewis defines Islam and in the chapter "The House of War" he reviews the various interpretations of jihad, defines martyrdom, and what it means to Muslims. Throughout the initial chapters, Lewis gives numerous historical examples which demonstrate what makes Islam unique and traces Islam's development through what he terms as "crusades to imperialism." Lewis shows how Islam is different from other world religions, specifically he states that "Islam is not a matter of faith and practice; it is also an identity and a loyalty--for many, an identity and a loyalty that transcends all others" (2003, 17).

After the first few chapters, Lewis begins to focus on the relationship between the US and the Islamic Middle East, specifically the history of anti-Americanism in the region. Lewis argues that Middle Eastern anti-Americanism took its roots during World

War II. He states that Nazi German influence throughout the region during this time produced an Arab society that perceived the US as, "the ultimate example of civilization without culture; materially advanced but soulless and artificial; technologically complex but without the spirituality and vitality of the rooted, human, national cultures of Germans and other 'authentic' peoples" (Lewis 2003, 70). Lewis further states that after the collapse of the Third Reich and the ending of German influence, anti-Americanism continued to fester within the region because another power and another philosophy, even more anti-American, took its place--the Soviet Union and its version of Marxism which denounced Western capitalism and most of all anything American.

Finally, Lewis continues by stating that the most recent cause of Arab Muslim anti-Americanism is the relationship between Israel and the US. Specifically, Lewis states that this now strategic alliance, which grew out of a response to the spread of Soviet influence in the Middle East, has caused this phenomenon to continue.

One of the leading Middle Eastern experts who often argues that the reason Americans are disliked within the Arab Muslim world is because there is a clash of cultures between the US and Arab Muslims, is the Pulitzer Prize winning author and *The New York Times* columnist Thomas L. Friedman. His book titled, *Longitudes and Latitudes: The World in the Age of Terrorism*, is a compilation of his *New York Times* columns and personal diary entries between 15 December 2000, and 20 April 2003. These columns and diary entries examine many issues ranging from US policy in the Middle East, the war in Afghanistan, and the rise of anti-Americanism around the world prior to and after 11 September 2001.

This book is not a history book but rather is Friedman's attempt to provide raw data to the people of the world as he traveled from New York to Jerusalem, Iraq, Pakistan, Saudi Arabia, India, and Belgium in the pursuit of understanding what people were thinking about during this volatile time in history. That is, Friedman wanted to capture the emotions of various groups of people, primarily non-US individuals, throughout the world and ensure their words were being heard.

Many of the columns and diary entries are interviews with high level political officials from various Middle Eastern nations, but the majority of the columns are written as a result of Friedman's conversations with everyday Arab Muslims. These columns and diary entries are the ones that provide insight into the true feelings Arab Muslims, as well as others, have about the US. For instance, after speaking to several Arab Muslim men. Friedman wrote, "They see America as the most powerful lethal weapon destroying their religious universe, or at least the universe they would like to build" (2003, 357).

Another source of vital information for this thesis is the book written by Andrew Kohut and Bruce Stokes titled, *America Against the World: How We are Different and Why We are Disliked.* This book utilizes the Pew Research Center's series of global opinion surveys to examine how the world views the US and its people. The authors use these polls to show how American attitudes and values have caused a rise in anti-American sentiment around the world.

The authors make the most of the global opinion surveys by reviewing world opinions about religion, democracy, globalization, culture, use of force, and US foreign policy. The authors then attempt to analyze these issues and determine if and how they impact anti-Americanism around the world.

Throughout the book, the authors argue that one of the main causes of anti-American sentiment is the American culture and others' misunderstanding of it. That is, what causes anti-American sentiment is the view that the American public's extreme individualism often results in Americans not concerning themselves with other people or other portions of the globe. Additionally, the authors argue that the US' pervasive religiosity and profound patriotism are often exaggerated and misunderstood by anti-American critics around the world. However, the authors also argue that many criticisms of the US arise out of misunderstandings or misinformation about what Americans actually feel or do.

The authors conclude that Americans hold values and thoughts that are very different than other people in the world and because of these differences, anti-Americanism is on the rise.

Another beneficial source that provides detailed information on Islamic ideology and Arab Muslim culture is the book, *Knowing the Enemy: Jihadist Ideology and the War on Terror* written by Professor Mary Habeck. This source mainly focuses on Islamic extremists groups whose ideologies are based on Islamic thinkers such as Muhammad ibn 'Adb al Wahhab, Hasan al-Banna, and Sayyid Qutb, but the book does provide useful insight into the greater Arab Muslim culture.

Although Dr. Habeck primarily focuses most of her work on the Islamic extremist ideology, she does reveal some of the underlying biases within the Muslim Arab world that cause anti-American sentiment. In the first portion of this book, Dr. Habeck examines the multiple interpretations of the Quran and hadith and shows why a majority of Muslims feel that these texts have implications beyond just their religious lives. For

25

example, she states that within the Arab Muslim world the Quran and hadith directly affect how people view democracy, capitalism, international organizations, human rights, rights of women, and religious tolerance. Therefore, due to these conflicting views, anti-American sentiment remains highly contagious within the region.

The last portion of the book, Dr. Habeck focuses exclusively on how the extremists interpret the Quran and hadith and how they use examples throughout history to demonstrate a Western assault on Islam. Specifically, she analyzes how extremists use these interpretations and historical examples to justify their overt hatred and terrorist actions against the West and especially the US.

An interesting resource used in researching this thesis was the book, *Why do People Hate America* written by Ziauddin Sardar and Merryl Wyn Davies. What makes this book so unique is that the authors utilize popular American television shows and movies like *The West Wing*, *Alias,* and *Mr. Smith Goes to Washington* to assist in demonstrating the American culture and way of thinking.

According to the authors, the purpose of the book was to argue that "hatred is never simple, one-way traffic. It is a relational, reactive condition" (Sardar and Davies 2004, xii). The authors argue that there are four main reasons for anti-American sentiment. The reasons are what the authors' term as: (1) Existential. The US has made it too difficult for other people to exist. That is, the US led globalization has resulted in the physical, political, economical, and cultural degradation of developing countries and their populations; (2) Cosmological. In today's globalized world the US is seen as the prime cause of everything. Thus because everything in the world has something to do with the US, if the US does not support it, it will not happen nor function; (3) Ontological. That is

26

bad versus good. Therefore, according to the US, everything that is good is directly related to the US and everything the US opposes is bad. For example, America is good and terrorist are evil; and (4) Definitions. America is the lone hyperpower in the world. Thus, the US defines what a democracy is and what is not, what is considered justice and what is considered injustice, what human rights are, who is a fundamentalist, and who is a terrorist.

This source provides a different examination into anti-American sentiment. However, similar to many regimes and influential groups within the Middle East, the authors provide only one side to their arguments. That is, the authors focus on American policies and how they negatively affect various people around the world but fail to demonstrate how these same policies benefit various other people around the world.

Finally, in regards to a clash between cultures, was an article published in the *European Journal of American Culture* written by Professor Richard Crockett titled "No common ground? Islam, anti-Americanism and the United States." This article further argues that Arab Muslim anti-American sentiment is caused by several factors including cultural conflict. In his article, Dr. Crocket does not focus on specifically identifying causes of Arab Muslim anti-Americanism but rather attempts to identify what areas of common ground exist between the US and the Arab Muslim world. Dr. Crocket examines this subject by developing two models he terms as "a cooperation model and a conflict model." Using these two models, Dr. Crocket suggests that it is not the conflict of cultures that gives rise to political conflict and war but political conflict and especially the collapse of political authority, which provokes cultural conflict (2004, 139).

Self-Interested Manipulation by Middle Eastern Governments or Influential Arab Groups

The final cause, argued in this thesis, is that Muslim Arab anti-American sentiment is also a product of self-interested manipulation by various groups within the Arab society that use anti-Americanism to distract public attention from other far more serious problems within the Arab Muslim society (Rubin 2002, 73). The review of the following literature focuses on how Arab governments and influential groups manipulate the Arab Muslim population in order to remain in power.

One of the leading experts to argue Arab Muslim anti-American sentiment is a product of self-interested manipulation is the director of the Global Research in International Affairs Center and Editor of the *Middle East Review of International Affairs Journal*, Barry Rubin. In his article published in the *Foreign Affairs Journal* "The Real Roots of Arab Anti-Americanism," Rubin demonstrates how failing political systems and movements within the Arab Muslim world use anti-Americanism to improve their standing among Arab Muslims. Rubin displays facts that show American support for Arab Muslims in eleven of twelve major conflicts in the past one-half century, while at the same time, he demonstrates how Arab anti-American leaders distort this record. Finally, Rubin argues that Arab Muslim rulers use anti-American sentiment to discourage political responsiveness, freedom of speech, and modernization.

Additionally, another article published in the *Brown Journal of World Affairs* titled "Anti-Americanism Re-Examined" written by Barry Rubin in conjunction with Judith Colp Rubin argues that Arab Muslim anti-American sentiment is a product of anti-American governments and influential groups using anti-Americanism to distract their societies from their shortcomings. Specifically, the authors argue that dictatorial regimes and Muslim clerics blame US interference in the region to explain the ever widening material gap between the West and themselves.

In the next chapter, the methodology utilized for this thesis will be illustrated. It will explain how the quantitative data will be displayed and describe how the facts will be investigated.

CHAPTER 3

RESEARCH METHODOLOGY

The highly negative attitude of much of the Arab world and the Muslim world towards the United States in the last few years represents the underlying source of threat to American national security, often referred to only by its overt manifestation in the war on terrorism (Fulton 2004, 1).

Stephen P. Cohen

Introduction

The purpose of this research is to identify the basis for Arab Muslim antipathy toward the US. This chapter delineates the methodology for identifying the extent of Arab Muslim antipathy and how this complex phenomenon was analyzed to determine this basis.

The research for this thesis began with a comprehensive review of the primary research question: Is Arab Muslim antipathy in the Middle East toward the US based on US policies in the region, specifically relating to the Israeli and Palestinian conflict? The research methodology used consisted of two distinct approaches, a quantitative approach followed by a qualitative approach. The quantitative approach was used to determine the history and extent of Arab Muslim antipathy toward the US. Once it was determined that there currently is a very high level of anti-American sentiment within the Arab world, the focus of the research moved to the qualitative approach to investigate the basis of this anti-American sentiment.

The qualitative approach gathered data, examined in the previous chapter, used to investigate the cause of Arab Muslim anti-American sentiment. In addition to providing data to answer the primary research question of this study, the qualitative approach also sought to identify any additional contributing factors and how each of the factors may possibly contribute to the growing Arab Muslim anti-American sentiment.

Quantitative Approach

The first approach directly pursued data in order to provide information about the opinions of Arab Muslims regarding to the US. This approach gathered statistics about Arab Muslim opinions from a variety of international public surveys to include the Pew Research Center for the People and the Press, Zogby International, World Public Opinion, British Broadcasting Corporation World Poll, and the Gallup Organization. These surveys provided a variety of quantitative statistics and assisted in determining the overall history and current extent of Arab Muslim anti-American sentiment.

As mentioned in chapter 1, this thesis is utilizing previously conducted surveys and is thus subject to each survey's specific questions, geographical locations, and internal computations. Therefore, because of this limitation, it is recognized that the data presented by these various organizations may be biased or slanted due to the sources of funding for each survey or possibly for political reasons. Additionally, it is also recognized that the data within these surveys may not be valid because of a variety of factors or threats to validity that include: statistical regression, how each survey selected the survey subjects, the history or external events that occurred between each survey and changes in the instruments, observers. or scorers which may have produced changes in outcomes. This thesis cannot directly affect these surveys but understands the limitations of utilizing this data in determining the overall extent of Arab Muslim antipathy toward the US.

In order to demonstrate the extent of Arab Muslim antipathy toward the US, this thesis will utilize the following four tables (see table 1 through table 4).

Table 1. Favorable Opinion of the United States

Country/Year	2002	2003	2004	2005	2006	2007
Jordan						
Lebanon						
Egypt						
Kuwait						
Palestinian Territory						

Table 2. Opinion of the United States

	2002		2005		2006	
	Fav	Unfav	Fav	Unfav	Fav	Unfav
Saudi Arabia						
Egypt						
Jordan						
Lebanon						

Table 3. Opinion of the US in 2005 Versus 2006

	Better	Worse	Same
Jordan			
Lebanon			
Saudi Arabia			
Egypt			

Table 4. Favorable View of American People

Country/ Year	2002	2003	2004	2005	2006	2007
Jordan						
Lebanon						
Egypt						
Kuwait						
Palestinian Territory						

Qualitative Approach

The principal method of analysis used to investigate possible answers to the

primary research question was to compare and contrast the data compiled from the

secondary opinion questions, asked by the various world opinion survey organizations, with the many different viewpoints about Arab Muslim anti-American sentiment reviewed in chapter 2. During this process, as each source of information was identified, the relevant facts, ideas, and points were extracted and sorted in accordance with the outline of this thesis. When the experts and the data did not agree about the causes of Arab Muslim anti-American sentiment, each viewpoint was evaluated and analyzed and eventually it was determined which viewpoint was better supported by historical, relevant facts, as well as, the data produced by the world opinion surveys.

As the number of sources grew and the analysis progressed, the importance of critical thinking and inductive reasoning increased. In the end, this thesis had compiled a vast amount of research, arguing a variety of viewpoints on the topic, and thus inductive reasoning became the primary method of answering the research question. The ability to unequivocally determine the basis for Arab Muslim antipathy toward the US is extremely difficult. Therefore, conclusions and recommendations derived from the research will be included in chapter 5.

Summary and Conclusion

Interest in this topic grew because of the writer's various experiences in the Middle East between 2000 and 2004. These experiences, combined with the fact that the most recent world opinion polls show how much Arab Muslims truly dislike the US demonstrate how important this topic is to the Long War. Most experts agree that in order for the US to succeed in the Long War, the US must have the support of the Arab Muslim population, and as of right now, the US does not have that support. Therefore, something must change.

This research represents a quest to identify the basis of this anti-American phenomenon and provide some innovative thought on why this phenomenon is so important to the US' efforts in the Long War. The next chapter will demonstrate the overall extent of Arab Muslim anti-American sentiment and investigate the basis of this extremely complex phenomenon.

CHAPTER 4

INTRODUCTION

I believe that America bears responsibility for all of Israel, both in its occupation of the lands or in all its settlements policies. America does not apply any pressure on Israel on par with the pressures it applies against the Palestinian Authority. America is a hypocritical nation when it comes to the question of Palestine: for it gives solid support and lethal weapons to the Israelis, but gives the Arabs and the Palestinians only words (Makdisi 2002, 555).

Sayyid Muhammad Husayn Fadlallah
A leading Shiite Muslim scholar and spiritual leader of Hezbollah

Introduction

This chapter is the core of this study. This chapter will display statistical data

demonstrating the overall extent of Arab Muslim antipathy toward the US. This chapter

will also analyze this data in an attempt to understand and explain this very complex

phenomenon, and will also address the primary research question of this thesis: Is Arab

Muslim antipathy in the Middle East toward the US based on US policies in the region,

specifically relating to the Israeli and Palestinian conflict?

While attempting to understand the complex phenomenon of Arab Muslim anti-

Americanism this chapter will also investigate and analyze two additional contributing

factors clashing cultures and self-interested manipulation by Middle Eastern governments

or influential Arab groups. This chapter will further analyze how these contributing

factors, in conjunction with US polices, directly affect the overall extent of the Arab

Muslim anti-American sentiment.

Anti-American sentiment within the Arab world is a young phenomenon but is

not entirely new. There is little doubt that anti-American sentiment currently exists within the Arab Muslim world but in order to analyze why this phenomenon exists one must first investigate how it came to be.

Historical Background

Not surprisingly, little was known about America throughout the eighteenth and nineteenth centuries in the Arab world. In fact, the first recorded mention of America as a political symbol in the Islamic world was in Istanbul on 14 July 1793 (Lewis 2003, 66). Throughout this timeframe, there were only a few scattered references of the US in the Arab world.

In the late nineteenth and early twentieth centuries, somewhat more attention was given to America; however, it was still extremely limited. Headlines and other references to the US were neither positive nor negative but seemed to focus on the many missionaries and their work in the region. These missionaries, although forbidden to proselytize Muslims, provided modern secondary and higher education to an ever growing number of boys and eventually girls throughout the region. Many missionaries were not necessarily liked because of their religious views but there did not seem to be any mistrust or outward hatred toward them. More importantly, these missionaries brought about a general feeling of favor and gratitude from a large portion of Arab Muslims.

The idea of a generous America reached its peak among Arab Muslims during and immediately following World War I. Americans were not only identified with educational efforts in the region but they were also essential to relief efforts amid a terrible famine in Beirut and the surrounding region. Additionally, President Wilson's proclamations on self-determination reinforced the belief among Arab nationalist that the

US was different from European powers, which had agreed to partition the postwar

Middle East into a variety of colonial outposts (Makdisi 2002, 544).

World War II, the oil industry, and postwar developments brought many more

Americans to the Arab world. At the same time, increasing numbers of Arab Muslims

began to travel to the US, first as students, then as businessmen, and eventually as

immigrants. Eventually, cinema and later television brought the American way of life, or

a certain version of it, to millions of Arab Muslims. Simultaneously, a wide range of

American products were introduced into a variety of Muslim markets, attracting new

customers and creating an assortment of new tastes and ambitions. During this era,

America represented freedom, justice, and opportunity as well as wealth, power, and

success, all at a time, when these qualities were not regarded as sins or crimes (Lewis

2003, 69).

America's overall standing within the Arab Muslim world began to change as the

Cold War gained momentum. The Cold War exacerbated any doubt felt by US policy

makers toward any potentially destabilizing force in the Middle East. For example, US

policy makers were unwilling to support Egypt's Gamal Abdel Nasser's Pan-Arab

rhetoric within the context of the recent history of European colonial exploitation of the

Arab world. Nasser saw the nation of Israel as the greatest threat to Arabs, whereas US

policy makers focused on the dangers of any Soviet intrusion into the Middle East. Thus,

US policy makers perceived Nasser within a Cold War logic that dismissed his attempt at

nonalignment and portrayed him as a dangerous, destabilizing, and radical Arab leader.

Specifically, US policy makers regarded his decision to seek arms from the eastern bloc

and his nationalization of the Suez Canal as destabilizing to pro-Western regimes in the region. In fact, in July 1958, 14,000 US troops were deployed to Lebanon in an attempt to stabilize the area in support of the pro-Western regime. These troops were sent to the region as a signal of US determination to ward off alleged radical Arab nationalism and Soviet expansionism. This politicization of the US on the side of conservative autocratic regimes fostered the first round of anti-American sentiment among Arab Muslims (Makdisi 2002, 549).

This new and developing anti-American sentiment was not characterized by a hatred of America, American things or the people of America but rather as a relatively new identification of American power and policies viewed as a force for repression rather than liberation in the Arab Muslim world. Nasser expressed this feeling in a speech he gave in 1958:

> America . . . engaged in a revolution in order to get rid of British colonialism and in order to raise the living standards across the US. . . . America refuses to see the reality of the situation in the Middle East and forgets its own history and its own revolution and its own logic. They fought colonialism as we fight colonialism. . . . How do they deny us our right to improve our condition just as they did theirs? I do not understand why they do not respect the will of the peoples of the Arab East? We call for positive neutrality. All the peoples of the Arab Middle East are set on non-alignment. Why should these peoples not have their way? Why is their will not respected? (Makdisi 2002, 549)

The secular, anti-imperialist rhetoric of various influential movements, Arab Muslim intellectuals, and progressive Arab Muslim governments now regarded the US as a representative of the historic force of colonialism and imperialism and as a power holding the Arab world back from its rightful place as an independent and influential power on the world stage. Anti-imperialist movements were equated with anti-American rhetoric and the US was seen as supporting allegedly retrograde regimes instead of the supposedly more progressive ones (Makdisi 2002, 549).

In the 1960s as Arab nationalism grew, secular, anti-imperialist, and at times anti-American expression prevailed throughout the region. But there also existed a feeling of Islamic dissidence from the autocratic governments of the Arab world. During this time, a religious revival began to gain momentum throughout the region. These very influential Islamists, unlike secularists, framed their politics as a response to the violation of an alleged tradition and envisioned a revival of a pure Islamic state and society. The leaders of this Islamic revival sought out and identified their enemies as the enemies of God and now regarded the US as a representative of evil, an opponent of all that is good and more importantly of Islam, specifically its culture, history, and civilization.

A key figure in the development of these new attitudes and the religious revival was the Egyptian, Sayyid Qutb, who became a leading ideologue of Muslim fundamentalism and an active member of the fundamentalist organization known as the Muslim Brotherhood. Qutb, who had once admired certain facets of the US, turned away from it because of its materialism and support for Israel. Qutb's callous analysis of Muslims as beleaguered sustained a firm yet influential Islamist interpretation of history and politics as an age-old clash of civilizations between the believers and their enemies. It was not freedom or temptation that Qutb opposed; it was what he saw as the degradation, corruption, injustice, authoritarianism and materialism imposed on Muslims by their enemies (Makdisi 2002, 550).

The Islamists alternative to the secular Arab nationalism was galvanized after Israel's success in the 1967 War and, just as important, when the US supported Shah of Iran was toppled in 1979 and replaced by an Islamic republic. As a result of these two very important events, an intense power struggle occurred between Islamists and secularists throughout the Arab world. After these events, many influential Arab Muslim leaders and groups denounced the US culture and called for all Arab Muslims to adhere to the proper Islamic codes of conduct. During this time, throughout the Arab Muslim world, Islamist movements entrenched themselves into national politics and remained an oppositional force to authoritarian governments as well as US influence and presence (Makdisi 2002, 551).

Throughout the 1980s and 1990s the US loomed ever more clearly as the unequivocal Middle Eastern regional hegemon; the US was the largest arms seller to the Middle East (particularly the gulf Arab states), an increasingly staunch supporter of Israel, and the guarantor of the authoritarian status quo (the wealthiest Arabs). Additionally, the US military firmly planted itself in Saudi Arabia following the 1991 Gulf War and oversaw stringent sanctions against the Iraqi regime. All of this, combined with the Iranian revolutionary upheaval and the defeat of the Soviets in Afghanistan, continued the rise of influence and importance of many Islamists. These Islamists came to see the US as a leader of a new crusade, a term that in the Arab world is replete not only with religious connotations of spiritual violations but equally with political ideas of occupation and oppression (Makdisi 2002, 552).

Extent of Arab Muslim Anti-Americanism

In Arab Muslim countries, anti-American sentiment is not only felt by a large portion of intellectuals but it is also felt throughout the masses. In these areas, traditional religion, oppressive politics and economic hardships combine to make anti-Americanism an extremely widespread response to a wide range of collective and personal frustrations and grievances. Anti-Americanism is extremely high in the Arab Muslim world and because of this, US efforts in the region continue to be affected.

Many recent world opinion surveys have shown that anti-American sentiment is high around the world, especially in Arab Muslim countries. The results of these surveys show that anti-Americanism is extensive and has been for the past several years (see tables 5, 6, and 7).

Table 5. Favorable Opinion of the United States

	2002	2003	2004	2005	2006	2007
Jordan	25%	1%	5%	21%	15%	20%
Lebanon	36%	27%	—	42%	31%	47%
Egypt	—	—	—	—	30%	21%
Kuwait	—	66%	—	—	—	46%
Palestinian Territory	—	0%	—	—	—	13%

Source: Pew Research Center, *Rising Environmental Concern in 47-Nation Survey: Global Unease with Major World Powers* (Washington, DC: Pew Research Center, 27 June 2007), 9, http://pewglobal.org/reports/display.php?ReportID=256 (accessed 2 July 2007).

Simultaneously, other international surveys show similar statistics relating to the levels of anti-American sentiment in the Arab Muslim world. These statistics also confirm that the level of anti-American sentiment within the Arab Muslim world has been and continues to be very high.

Table 6. Opinion of the United States

	2002		2005		2006	
	Fav	Unfav	Fav	Unfav	Fav	Unfav
Saudi Arabia	12%	87%	9%	89%	12%	82%
Egypt	15%	76%	14%	85%	14%	83%
Jordan	34%	61%	33%	62%	5%	90%
Lebanon	26%	70%	32%	60%	28%	68%

Source: Zogby International, Five Nation Survey of the Middle East, Submitted to: Arab American Institute, December 2006, 3, http://aai.3cdn.net/96d8eeaec55ef4c217_ m9m6b97wo.pdf (accessed 2 July 2007).

Table 7. Opinion of the US in 2005 versus 2006

	Better	Worse	Same
Jordan	1%	76%	22%
Lebanon	10%	47%	40%
Saudi Arabia	9%	62%	28%
Egypt	4%	72%	18%

Source: Zogby International, Five Nation Survey of the Middle East, Submitted to: Arab American Institute, December 2006, 3, http://aai.3cdn.net/96d8eeaec55ef4c217_ m9m6b97wo.pdf (accessed 2 July 2007).

The statistics in tables above reveal the extreme levels of anti-American sentiment within the Arab Muslim world. Additionally, world opinion polls also show that Arab

Muslims have very little confidence in the US. That is, most Arab Muslims have very little confidence in the abilities of the US to promote peace, establish stability in the region, or provide more economic assistance. In fact, according to a survey conducted by the University of Maryland and Zogby International over 69 percent of Arab Muslims stated that they have very little confidence in the US and only 3 percent stated they had a lot of confidence in the US (2006). Additionally, the same survey also showed that a majority (57 percent) of Arab Muslims reportedly have a "Very Unfavorable" view of the US while an extremely large percentage (4 percent) reportedly has a "Very Favorable" view of the US (see figure 1).

How can these statistics be explained? Can these statistics be explained by simply stating that Arab Muslims are upset or disappointed with the US because of US actions in the region? Arab Muslim anti-Americanism is not that simple and thus there must be something more.

DUE TO COPYRIGHT RESTRICTIONS,

IMAGES ARE NOT INCLUDED

IN THIS ELECTRONIC EDITION.

Figure 1. Favorable Attitudes Toward the United States
Source: Anwar Sadat Chair for Peace and Development, University of Maryland/Zogby International, 2006 Annual Arab Public Opinion Survey, A Six Country Study: Egypt, Jordan, Lebanon, Morocco, Saudi Arabia (KSA), and UAE, http://www.bsos.umd.edu/sadat/2006%20Arab%20Public%20Opinion%20Survey.ppt (accessed on 9 August 2007).

Basis and Contributing Factors of Arab Muslim Anti-American Sentiment

Arab Muslim anti-American sentiment is a very difficult phenomenon to explain. There really is no one defining cause or explanation. Therefore, in order to understand this growing phenomenon, one must first examine the basis of this anti-American sentiment and then determine what other factors contribute to this phenomenon that is so widespread and intense throughout the Middle Eastern region.

The Basis

Statistics confirm that the basis of Arab Muslim anti-American sentiment is the

US foreign policy in the region, especially as it relates to the Israeli and Palestinian

conflict. Many Arab Muslims resent the US because of what they feel are policies that

range from disregard to Palestinian rights and blind support of Israel, to support of puppet

dictatorial regimes, to inhumane sanctions against Iraq, and the American led war and

follow-on occupation of Iraq (see table 8) (Battah 2006). Such policies breed resentment

toward the US and its supporters in the region. It is these policies that must be analyzed

to determine how they form the basis for the current high levels of anti-American

sentiment in the Arab world.

Table 8. Source of Attitude Toward United States

	Jordan	Lebanon	Saudi Arabia	UAE	Egypt
American Values	16%	9%	10%	9%	<1%
American Policy	76%	80%	86%	75%	90%
Not Sure	7%	11%	6%	16%	<1%

Source: Anwar Sadat Chair for Peace and Development, University of Maryland/Zogby
International, 2006 Annual Arab Public Opinion Survey, A Six Country Study: Egypt,
Jordan, Lebanon, Morocco, Saudi Arabia (KSA), and UAE, http://www.bsos.umd.edu/
sadat/2006%20Arab%20Public%20Opinion%20Survey.ppt (accessed on 9 August 2007).

Arab Muslim Anti-Americanism and United States Regional Policies

As the US gained influence within the Arab Muslim world many Arab Muslims

began to resent the US because of its policies in the Middle Eastern region. Arab

Muslims came to see the US as the main arbitrator of war as well as peace in the region. Additionally, many Arab Muslims considered the way the US pursued its own interest during the Cold War as extremely detrimental to the Arab region and more importantly its people. Foremost among the Arab Muslim grievances about US policy in the region were, and in many cases still are its: anti-Arab nationalist posture in the 1950s and 1960s; the consistent anti-Arab bias in the Israeli conflict and alleged obstructionist role in the peace process; imposition of severe sanctions against the people of Iraq and more recent military aggression against Iraq and the perceived subsequent occupation of an Arab Muslim country; the stationing of troops on Arab lands, and propping up of puppet regimes. A number of these factors are long-standing grievances, that along with new ones add up to a perceived image of the US as a dedicated and implacable foe of Arab sovereignty and rights. These actions leave little room for many Arab Muslims to believe that America enacts its regional policies with their best interest in mind (Battah 2006).

The US, in the view of many Arab Muslims, is guilty of a "double standard" in terms of its regional policies. For example, one country, Israel, contravenes one UN Security Council resolution after another concerning the occupation of territory by force, yet receives nearly $3 billion a year in military and civilian aid from Washington. This is the largest grant by the US to any country, amounting to roughly $5 hundred per Israeli, more than the total Gross National Product per capita of many African countries struggling to obtain relief from crushing international debts (La Guardia 2003, 380).

Simultaneously, another country, Iraq, contravenes UN resolutions arising from its invasion of Kuwait, yet languishes a decade after the liberation of Kuwait under the most comprehensive sanctions devised by the international community, resulting in poverty, disease, and premature death for many Arab Muslims (La Guardia, 2003, 380).

Saddam was denounced for oppressing his own people, but the daily bloodletting in Israel and Palestine is all but forgotten. In his State of the Union address in 2003, President Bush declared that "the gravest danger in the war on terror, the gravest danger facing America and the world is outlaw regimes that seek and possess nuclear, chemical, and biological weapons." He barely mentioned the issue that concerns Arab Muslims most closely, saying: "In the Middle East, we will continue to seek peace between a secure Israel and a democratic Palestine" (La Guardia 2003, 380).

It is these policies and a belief in a "double standard" that bother Arab Muslims the most. To many Arab Muslims, America's malicious influence is all pervasive: its military power fragments the Arab nation, its money corrupts Arab rulers, and its social manners pollute Islam. In this climate of heightened resentment, anyone who can humiliate or stand up to the US is regarded as a hero to a substantial number of Arab Muslims (La Guardia 2003, 381).

To illustrate how Arab Muslims feel about the US and its policies, table 9 reveals that most Arab Muslims do not think that the US cares or even tries to take into account other countries interest when determining and executing its foreign policies.

Table 9. Interest of Other Countries

In making policy decisions, to what extent do you think the US takes into account the interest of other countries

Country	Year	Great Deal	Fair Amount	No too Much	Not at All	Don't Know
Egypt	2007	12%	12%	33%	41%	1%
Jordan	2007	8%	15%	43%	32%	2%
	2005	5%	12%	41%	41%	1%
	2004	1%	15%	38%	39%	7%
	2003	3%	16%	44%	36%	1%
	2002	7%	21%	35%	36%	1%
Kuwait	2007	8%	22%	22%	42%	5%
	2003	27%	34%	20%	15%	4%
Lebanon	2007	6%	28%	32%	33%	1%
	2005	13%	22%	27%	30%	8%
	2003	5%	13%	36%	45%	1%
	2002	4%	16%	28%	50%	3%
Palestinian Territory	2007	5%	7%	26%	57%	5%
	2003	1%	5%	31%	61%	2%

Source: Pew Research Center, *Rising Environmental Concern in 47-Nation Survey: Global Unease with Major World Powers* (Washington, DC: Pew Research Center, 27 June 2007), 9, http://pewglobal.org/reports/display.php?ReportID=256 (accessed 2 July 2007).

Arab Muslim Anti-Americanism and United States Support for Israel

On no issue is Arab anger at the US more widely and acutely felt than that of Palestine. For it is over Palestine that Arab secularist and Islamist interpretations of history unite in a common view of a massive gap separating official American declarations of support for freedom from actual American policies. There are very few accounts of anti-Americanism in the Arab world that do not address the Arab interpretation of US perceived uneven support for Israel over the Palestinians or other Arab Muslims in the Middle East.

Viewed from a Western perspective, the creation of Israel represented Jewish national redemption. But from an Arab perspective, Israel never has been and never could have been so understood. Zionism in Palestine, a land whose overwhelming majority was Arab at the turn of the twentieth century and for over a thousand years before that, caused the destruction of Palestinian society and the dispossession of its Arab inhabitants (Makdisi 2002, 553).

President Harry Truman quickly recognized Israel as the de facto authority in the territories it occupied in May 1948. However, it was not the US but rather the Soviet Union that ensured Israel's survival during those critical early months. In fact, it was weapons supplied by the Soviet Union, not the US, who took a neutral stance in the conflict, which allowed Israel to defeat the Arab armies in 1948.

In the following decade as the Cold War gained momentum, Israel drifted toward the US as several influential Arab Muslim countries allied themselves to the Soviet Union. After the Suez War of 1956, in which President Eisenhower intervened forcefully and decisively to secure the withdrawal of the Israeli, British, and French forces, the US-

Israeli relationship quickly continued to improve. The spread of Soviet influence in the Middle East and the enthusiastic response to it encouraged the US to look more favorable on Israel, who was seen as a reliable and a potentially useful ally in a largely hostile region (Lewis 2003, 97).

John F. Kennedy was the first president to guarantee Israel's security, and he sold Hawk anti-aircraft batteries to Israel in 1962. Lyndon B. Johnson, who prevaricated in the build-up to the Six Day War because of America's commitment to Vietnam, later sold fighter jets to Israel (La Guardia 2003, 377).

After the Israeli victory and the humiliation of the Arabs in 1967, both Israel and the Arabs were completely drawn into the Cold War. Israel rearmed with better and more plentiful weapons from the US, while the Arabs quickly rebuilt their forces with the assistance of the Soviet Union. Military incidents multiplied after 1969, when Egypt declared that it no longer recognized the ceasefire that ended the 1967 War and escalated into a campaign of increasingly severe border clashes dubbed the "War of Attrition" (La Guardia 2003, 126).

The 1973 Arab-Israeli War or the Yom Kippur War increased the US' involvement in the Middle East. The US carried out an emergency airlift of military supplies that helped Israel turn the tide of the war, but then prevented the Israeli army from completely crushing Egypt's Third Army. The US could not allow the defeat of its Israeli ally but at the same time could not permit the humiliation of Egypt (La Guardia 2003, 378).

This strategy, combined with Henry Kissinger's "shuttle diplomacy" in 1973, ultimately led the way for the Egyptian-Israeli peace treaty of 1978. After the signing of

51

the Camp David Accords, the US provided Egypt with aid almost as enormous as that given to Israel, approximately $2 billion a year compared with $3 billion for Israel. Thus in the 1970s and beyond, the US, despite its support for Israel, established itself as the only broker of peace in the region (La Guardia 2003, 378).

It was President Ronald Reagan who, seeing the world strictly divided into two parts, communists and anticommunists, formally elevated Israel as the US' "strategic ally" only months before it invaded Lebanon (La Guardia, 2003 378). US support for Israel continued throughout the Reagan administration, as the US adopted a policy of strong overt support for Israel, inaction against Israeli aggression against Arab Muslims and status quo preservation as long as it favored Israel. During the Regan administration, the US was able to compel an occupied Lebanon to sign a peace agreement with Israel and force the Palestinian Liberation Organization (PLO) to unilaterally recognize Israel in 1988.

The Israeli and Middle Eastern policies adopted by the US under President Reagan would most likely have continued during the George H. Bush administration had it not been for the Iraqi invasion of Kuwait in 1990. The 1991 Gulf War brought the Israeli-US relationship to the forefront. During this crisis many Arab Muslims began to feel that US policies in the region, especially in reference to the Israeli and Palestinian conflict, were hypercritical. Recognizing this growing trend, President Bush convened an international conference in Madrid, the Madrid Conference, in an attempt to solve the Arab-Israeli conflict. However, the results of the conference were more of the same; no true resolution to the conflict. In fact, the conference may have fractionated the conflict even further by establishing separate bilateral and multilateral approaches to solving the various and intense issues.

It seemed for a while as if the transformation of the world after the collapse of the Soviet Union and the crisis in the Gulf would weaken the long friendship between the US and Israel, which was established during the years of the Cold War when Israel was seen as a western bastion against Soviet expansionism. However, the relationship between Israel and the US was not put to the test for years to follow (La Guardia 2003, 378).

In 1993, President Bill Clinton was the fortunate heir of the Oslo accords, an agreement negotiated by the Israelis and the PLO without any US involvement. The Oslo accords were the first agreement to attain any true progress in the ongoing Israeli and Palestinian conflict. However, because this agreement was signed in Washington, the US again became the main broker of peace and stability in the region.

Oslo was renegotiated in 1995 and later seen as a useless and counterproductive framework. According to some Arab Muslims, Oslo II was urged to be "rolled back" by the neoconservatives in the US. It was this strong influence and Arial Sharon's provocative visit to the Temple Mount in September 2000 that all but killed Oslo II. President Clinton's last minute "parameters" were really insignificant in any efforts to solve the growing tension between the people of Israel and the Palestinians.

The George W. Bush administration would not have any interest in President Clinton's parameters or on any other Middle Eastern peace plan. In fact, President Bush was perceived as taking very little interest in being proactive in the Israeli and Palestinian continuing conflict. President Bush has supported an independent Palestinian state and did introduce what he termed the "roadmap" for peace. However, due to the War or

Terror and the war in Iraq, the Bush administration has not placed much emphasize on attempting to change the status quo in terms of the Israeli and Palestinian conflict.

For instance, the current administration publicly supported Israel during the most recent conflict in Lebanon. Additionally, the Bush administration, which has aggressively pursued democratic reforms in the Middle East, has refused to recognize the democratically elected HAMAS party after HAMAS won the parliamentary elections in January 2006. Specifically, President Bush said, "The US does not support political parties that want to destroy our ally Israel" (CNN.com 2006).

This record of support for Israel does not go unnoticed by Arab Muslims. Nor do the billions of dollars of annual aid to Israel or the American made and supplied missiles, helicopters, or fighter planes. Many Arab Muslims take notice of the political battles the US wages in the UN Security Council on behalf of Israel. Of the fifty-nine unilateral vetoes cast by the US during the period of 1972 to 2006, forty-one were cast to avert criticism against Israel or attempts to force Israel to consolidate its occupation of various disputed territories. Over the years, administration after administration has sought to redefine this conflict in support of Israel. Thus it is of little surprise that many Arab Muslims view that Israel is little more than the spearhead of American imperialism (Battah 2006).

Recent opinion polls confirm that many Arab Muslims feel that US policies strongly favor Israel over the Palestinians and other Arab countries (see table 10). This feeling adds to the already intense anti-American sentiment in the region. In fact, when asked how important the role of US policy toward the Arab-Israeli dispute was in developing attitudes of the US a majority of respondents in Jordan (58 percent), Lebanon

(52 percent), UAE (69 percent) and Egypt (90 percent) stated that it was extremely important. Saudi Arabia (38 percent) was the only country where a majority of respondents stated it was not extremely important (Anwar Sadat Chair for Peace and Development, University of Maryland/Zogby International, 2006).

Table 10. Opinion of United States Policies in Reference to Israel and Palestine

What's your opinion of US policies in the Middle East – would you say they are fair or do the favor Israel too much or do they favor the Palestinians too much

Country	Year	Fair	Favor Israel	Favor Palestinians	Don't Know
Egypt	2007	7%	86%	0%	7%
Jordan	2007	3%	91%	1%	5%
	2003	1%	99%	0%	0%
Kuwait	2007	4%	86%	5%	6%
	2003	14%	77%	1%	8%
Lebanon	2007	7%	89%	2%	2%
	2003	5%	90%	1%	3%
Palestinian Territory	2007	2%	90%	4%	4%
	2003	0%	96%	2%	2%

Source: Pew Research Center, *Rising Environmental Concern in 47-Nation Survey: Global Unease with Major World Powers* (Washington, DC: Pew Research Center, 27 June 2007), 54, http://pewglobal.org/reports/display.php?ReportID=256 (accessed 2 July 2007).

Why Palestine?

Everything in Israel and Palestine is larger than life. It is a sliver of a country-no more than 75 miles wide by 260 miles long, with a population of five million Jews and about four million Palestinians in both Israel and the occupied territories. Yet it commands the devotion of one billion Muslims, 1.7 billion Christians, and some 13 million Jews around the world (La Guardia 2003, 10). Why?

From an Arab Muslim point of view, the Jewish state symbolizes everything that they believe is wrong with their universe--cowardly and corrupt leaders, oppressive but incompetent armed forces and fragmentation of the Arab and Islamic nation. In short a state of weakness that allows foreigners to take Arab land with impunity (La Guardia 2003, xvii).

Additionally, Palestine has a deep religious meaning for many Arab Muslims. For many Muslims, Palestine is a *waqf*, or Islamic endowment, a sacred possession given in perpetuity. Many Arab Muslims believe that there can never be another sovereignty and Muslims are duty-bound to fight Israel (La Guardia 2003, 56).

At the same time, world opinion polls show that many Arab Muslims do in fact identify with many of the Palestinians and feel that the Palestinian issue is extremely important and is a very high priority (see figure 2). In fact, when asked how important US policy on the Arab-Israeli conflict was in developing their attitudes of the US over 50 percent of the respondents stated in was "extremely important", 11 percent said it was "important", 4 percent said it was "somewhat important" and 10 percent said it was "not important" (Anwar Sadat Chair for Peace and Development, University of Maryland and Zogby International 2006).

DUE TO COPYRIGHT RESTRICTIONS,

IMAGES ARE NOT INCLUDED

IN THIS ELECTRONIC EDITION.

Figure 2. Importance of Palestine in your Priorities
Source: Anwar Sadat Chair for Peace and Development, University of Maryland/Zogby International, 2006 Annual Arab Public Opinion Survey, A Six Country Study: Egypt, Jordan, Lebanon, Morocco, Saudi Arabia (KSA), and UAE, http://www.bsos.umd.edu/sadat/2006%20Arab%20Public%20Opinion%20Survey.ppt (accessed on 9 August 2007).

Finally, another important reason for the primacy of Palestine is that it is the licensed grievance in the region. The Palestinian issue is the only issue that can be freely and safely expressed in many Arab Muslim countries where the media are either wholly owned or strictly overseen by the government. Israel serves as a useful stand-in for complaints about the economic privation and political repression under which most Arab Muslims live and as a way of deflecting the resulting anger (Lewis 2003, 93).

Contributing Factors

Arab Muslim anti-Americanism can not be explained by simply stating that it is caused by the US policies in the region. This sentiment must also be viewed in conjunction with other contributing factors. The two other contributing factors are what can be termed as clashing cultures and self interested manipulation by Middle Eastern governments or influential Arab groups. It is these two contributing factors, combined with US policies, which causes this complex anti-American phenomenon.

Clashing Cultures

The first contributing factor that assists in explaining the high levels of anti-American sentiment in the Arab world is value based and according to University of Harvard professor, Samuel Huntington represents a "clash of civilizations." This clash between the West and the world is made more evident by the weakening of the nation-state, the emergence of indigenous anti-Western elite and international regionalism. Resurgent religion, like Islam, steps in to fill the void and thus cultural identities and interests become increasingly more important. It is the clash between two separate and different cultures, the West or Christianity and Islam, which has contributed to the growing anti-American sentiment in the Arab World.

In order to analyze the clash between these two civilizations, one must first determine if an Arab Muslim civilization exist and if it does exists, its importance. Once one determines the presence and importance of an Arab Muslim civilization then one can investigate how the relationships between these two civilizations can cause this deep resentment.

Arab Muslim Civilization

As stated previously, the Arab Muslim civilization is the notion of being Muslim before being identified as something else. It is a civilization that is composed of Arab Muslims who identify themselves first as Muslims and second as Jordanians, Saudis, or Egyptians. It is the belief that Islam, with all its practices, cultures, and beliefs comes before nationalism. That is, all Arab Muslims are united together; they are members of one larger Arab Muslim civilization. To them, national borders are only lines drawn on a map and only constrain the true Arab Muslim civilization.

The importance of Islam in everyday life throughout the Arab world is increasing. In many countries large percentages of the people think of themselves first as a Muslim rather than a citizen of a particular country. In fact, figure 3 demonstrates that many Arab Muslims find their basic identity and loyalty in terms of a religious identity rather than by ethnic or territorial criteria.

```
DUE TO COPYRIGHT RESTRICTIONS,

IMAGES ARE NOT INCLUDED

IN THIS ELECTRONIC EDITION.
```

Figure 3.   How Arab Muslims Identify Themselves
Source: Anwar Sadat Chair for Peace and Development, Arab Attitudes Toward Political and Social Issues, Foreign Policy and the Media, A Public Opinion Poll conducted jointly by the Anwar Sadat Chair for Peace and Development at the University of Maryland and Zogby International, May 2004, http://www.bsos.umd.edu/sadat/pub/Arab%20 Attitudes%20Towards%20Political%20and%20Social%20Issues,%20Foreign%20Policy %20and%20the%20Media.htm (accessed on 18 June 2007).

Additionally, a more recent survey illustrated below (see figure 4) confirms the

data from figure 3 in that many Arab Muslims tend to identify themselves as Muslim

before identifying themselves Arabs or citizens of a country.

DUE TO COPYRIGHT RESTRICTIONS,

IMAGES ARE NOT INCLUDED

IN THIS ELECTRONIC EDITION.

Figure 4.   Aspects of Self or Identity
Source: Anwar Sadat Chair for Peace and Development, University of Maryland/Zogby
International, 2006 Annual Arab Public Opinion Survey, A Six Country Study: Egypt,
Jordan, Lebanon, Morocco, Saudi Arabia (KSA), and UAE, http://www.bsos.umd.edu/
sadat/2006%20Arab%20Public%20Opinion%20Survey.ppt (accessed on 9 August 2007).

These polls verify what Bernard Lewis stated in his book *The Crisis of Islam: Holy War and Unholy Terror* that, "The higher level of religious faith and practice among Muslims as compared with followers of other religions is part of the explanation of the unique Muslim attitudes. It is not the whole explanation, since the same attitude may be found in individuals and even whole groups whose commitments to religious faith and practice is at best perfunctory. Islam is not only a matter of faith and practice; it is also an identity and a loyalty--for many, an identity and a loyalty that transcends all others" (2003, 17).

Furthermore, not only do statistics illustrate that many Arab Muslim identify themselves first as a Muslim but also these statistics reveal that an Islamic Resurgence has been increasing over the past several years (see figure 5). That is to say, recently, many more Arab Muslims are turning to Islam as a source of identity, meaning, stability, legitimacy, development, power and hope. According to Huntington, the Islamic Resurgence is the latest phase in the adjustment of Islamic civilization to the West (1996, 110).

Statistics such as those previously shown confirm that the Arab Muslim civilization currently exists and that this civilization is rapidly growing within the Arab world. Thus, since the Arab Muslim civilization exist, why then is there a clash between the Arab Muslim civilization and the West?

DUE TO COPYRIGHT RESTRICTIONS,

IMAGES ARE NOT INCLUDED

IN THIS ELECTRONIC EDITION.

Figure 5. Recent Historical Trends of Self or Identity
Source: Anwar Sadat Chair for Peace and Development, University of Maryland/Zogby International, 2006 Annual Arab Public Opinion Survey, A Six Country Study: Egypt, Jordan, Lebanon, Morocco, Saudi Arabia (KSA), and UAE, http://www.bsos.umd.edu/sadat/2006%20Arab%20Public%20Opinion%20Survey.ppt (accessed on 9 August 2007).

The Clash between the United States and Arab Muslims

If anti-American sentiment is somewhat common throughout the world why is it so rampant in the Arab Muslim world? Are these cultures so different? Do these two opposing cultures actually clash or can these cultures co-exist?

According to Huntington the basic ingredients that fuel the conflict between the US and the Arab Muslim world are the cultures that exist within each of these regions.

He argues that the underlying problem for the West is not Islamic fundamentalism but rather Islam itself. He further writes that Islam is a civilization whose people are convinced of the superiority of their culture and who are obsessed with the inferiority of their power. Huntington also states that the clash occurs because the people within the Western civilization are convinced of the universality of their culture and believe that their superior, if declining, power imposes on them the obligation to extend that culture throughout the world (1996, 218). Thus, according to these defining characteristics, these are two civilizations that will constantly be opposed because of the struggle for cultural superiority. Therefore, it is easy to deduce why Arab Muslims would be very wary and opposed to US norms and beliefs of individualism, freedoms, and democratic forms of government. Recent statistics also support the idea that many Arab Muslims feel it is not a good thing that American ideas and customs are spreading throughout the region (see table 11).

Table 11.   Spreading of American Ideas and Customs

Which comes closer to your view? Its good that American ideas and customs* are spreading here, or its bad that American ideas and customs are spreading here

Country	Year	It's Good	It's Bad	Don't Know
Egypt	2007	13%	79%	8%
Jordan	2007	12%	81%	7%
	2003	5%	93%	2%
	2002	13%	82%	6%
Kuwait	2007	10%	85%	5%
	2003	13%	79%	8%
Lebanon	2007	38%	58%	3%
	2003	31%	65%	4%
	2002	26%	67%	6%
Palestinian Territory	2007	3%	90%	7%
	2003	4%	94%	2%

* The terms American ideas and customs were not defined by the Pew Research Center.

Source: Pew Research Center, *Rising Environmental Concern in 47-Nation Survey: Global Unease with Major World Powers* (Washington, DC: Pew Research Center, 27 June 2007), http://pewglobal.org/reports/display.php?ReportID=256 (accessed 2 July 2007).

Additionally, statistics from multiple opinion polls show that the recent Islamic Resurgence and the ever increasing importance of Islam in various aspects of Arab

Muslim life, especially politics, have caused many Arab Muslims to redefine the importance of their religion, culture, and values (see tables 12 and 13). Surveys reveal that large majorities in Jordan (97 percent) and Lebanon (54 percent) welcome the idea of Islam playing a greater role in people's lives. Additionally, of those who see Islam playing a greater role attribute it to the growing immorality in their society as well as pointing to concerns about Western influence (Pew Research Center 2005b, 22).

Table 12.   Role of Clergy in the Political System

Which statement do you agree with more?					
	Jordan	Lebanon	Saudi Arabia	UAE	Egypt
"Religion must be respected, but clergy should not dictate the political system."	36%	50%	33%	25%	50%
"Clergy must play a greater role in our political system."	42%	28%	48%	45%	47%
Neither	16%	22%	19%	21%	2%

Source: Anwar Sadat Chair for Peace and Development, Arab Attitudes Toward Political and Social Issues, Foreign Policy and the Media. A Public Opinion Poll conducted jointly by the Anwar Sadat Chair for Peace and Development at the University of Maryland and Zogby International, May 2004, 5, http://www.bsos.umd.edu/sadat/pub/Arab%20 Attitudes%20Towards%20Political%20and%20Social%20Issues,%20Foreign%20Policy %20and%20the%20Media.htm (accessed on 18 June 2007).

Today many Arab Muslims are rejecting American influence upon local society and politics. Arab Muslims are rejecting US values and institutions. Many today are stressing the need to maintain the integrity of their culture against what they consider the American onslaught. Arab Muslims fear and resent US power and the threat which it poses to their society and beliefs. Arab Muslims see the American culture as materialistic, corrupt, decadent, and immoral. At the same time, they also see it as seductive and hence stress all the more the need to resist its impact on their way of life. Increasingly, Arab Muslims attack the US not for adhering to an imperfect religion but for not adhering to any religion at all (Huntington 1996, 213). In fact, according to a survey conducted by the Pew Research Center in 2005, over 95 percent of Jordanians and 61 percent of Lebanese believe that Americans are not religious enough (Pew Research Center 2005a, 16).

Table 13.   Amount of Role Clergy Play in Politics

When you look at Arab countries today and think about government and politics, do you feel the clergy play too much of a role, too little a role, or is their role just about right?					
	Jordan	**Lebanon**	**Saudi Arabia**	**UAE**	**Egypt**
Too much	17%	20%	3%	5%	16%
Too little	55%	44%	49%	55%	45%
Just right	16%	28%	46%	20%	38%

Source: University of Maryland and Zogby International World Opinion Poll, Arab Attitudes toward Political and Social Issues, Foreign Policy and the Media, May 2004, 6, http://www.bsos.umd.edu/sadat/pub/Arab%20Attitudes%20Towards%20Political%20and%20Social%20Issues,%20Foreign%20Policy%20and%20the%20Media.htm (accessed on 18 June 2007).

Finally, recent statistics also illustrate a growing trend toward unfavorable opinions of Americans (see table 14). That is, Arab Muslims not only have unfavorable opinions of the US and its policies but also have unfavorable opinions of American people.

Table 14.   Favorable View of American People

Country/ Year	2002	2003	2004	2005	2006	2007
Jordan	53%	18%	21%	34%	39%	36%
Lebanon	47%	62%	—	66%	—	69%
Egypt	—	—	—	36%	36%	31%
Kuwait	—	71%	—	—	—	62%
Palestinian Territory	—	6%	—	—	—	21%

Source: Pew Research Center, *Rising Environmental Concern in 47-Nation Survey: Global Unease with Major World Powers* (Washington, DC: Pew Research Center, 27 June 2007), 12, http://pewglobal.org/reports/display.php?ReportID=256 (accessed 2 July 2007).

The clash of cultures explanation can not stand alone when trying to explain what causes Arab Muslim antipathy toward the US. However, as these statistics show, it does significantly contribute to the high levels of anti-American sentiment in the Arab Muslim world. It is this clash, that when combined with what the US does in the region and the manipulation of information by Arab Muslims governments and influential groups, that results in the extreme levels of anti-Americanism in the region.

<u>Self Interested Manipulation by Middle Eastern Governments or Influential Arab Groups</u>

The second contributing factor that assists in explaining the high levels of anti-American sentiment in the Arab world is most apparent among the ruling elites who find it easier to rationalize all their faults and failures by blaming them on external powers. That is, Arab Muslim governments and other very influential Arab Muslim groups distort information in order to deflect the masses attention away from their shortcomings and thus are able to focus their citizens' anger and frustration on external enemies such as the US or Israel.

In a region where most Arab Muslims are excluded from power and where official pronouncements are not to be trusted, the world is often interpreted through the rumor mill and conspiracy theories. The belief in great foreign plots and unseen forces helps to explain why the Arab Muslim nations appear to be so debilitated and allows them to shift responsibility away from their failures (La Guardia 2003, xix).

Arab Muslim leaders have encouraged their press to print the worst lies about America, as well as blatant anti-Jewish and Holocaust-denial articles, as a way of deflecting their people's anger away from them. That is why these regimes can now cooperate with the US only in secret. They have additionally let their conspiracy theories about America and Israel become easy excuses for why they never have to look at themselves--why they never have to ask: How is it that we had this incredible windfall of oil wealth and have done so poorly at building societies that can tap the vast potential of our people? (Friedman 2003, 133).

Does the Arab Muslim press actually produce publications that cause anti-American sentiment? The answer to that question is yes. For example, in late 2001 an editorial in the semiofficial Egyptian daily, Al-Ahram, written by Egypt's leading editor, who was personally appointed by Mubarak, Ibrahim Nafie, said that the US was deliberately making humanitarian food drops in areas in Afghanistan full of land mines. He also stated, "There have been several reports that the US humanitarian materials have been genetically treated with the aim of affecting the health of the Afghan people. If this is true, the US is committing a crime against humanity by giving the Afghan people hazardous humanitarian products" (Friedman 2003, 66).

Another aspect of this contributing factor is the strategy by various Arab Muslim regimes to give free hand in the expression of anti-Americanism as a way to demonstrate that such regimes are not "puppets" of the US. This is especially the case with the so-called pro-Western regimes, as they are more vulnerable to charges of treason and complicity. For such regimes, this is a necessary strategy of survival. They can accommodate US demands in order to continue to receive support but they have to walk a fine line. This has made such rulers adept at conceding to American requests in private but denying granting such request in public. For example, both Jordan and Saudi Arabia aided US war efforts against Iraq in 2003, while at the same time, criticized the war in public (Battah 2006).

Another example of this type of strategy exercised by Arab Muslim regimes in order to remain in power would be in Egypt. Specifically, Egyptian President Hosni Mubarak and other influential Egyptian leaders who are unable to deliver what they promised (jobs, housing, health care, or a future) devote enormous energy to distracting and deceiving their citizens. For over twenty years now, President Mubarak has been kept afloat by US assistance, which in 2002 totaled over $2 billion. Yet Mubarak has taken to jailing or threatening critics accused of accepting money from American foundations. The carefully monitored public film and television industries, meanwhile, still thrive on tales of evil Israeli conspiracies, reviving even the discredited tsarist forgery purporting to detail a conspiracy by Jews to seize control of the world or the Protocols of the Elders of Zion (Power and Dickey 2002).

The final facet that contributes to this specific contributing factor of Arab Muslim anti-American sentiment is the fact that almost the entire Arab Muslim region is affected by poverty and according to many various forms of tyranny. Both of these problems are attributed, especially by governments and other influential groups who need to divert attention away from themselves, to the US. In particular, regional poverty is linked to US economic dominance, now called "globalization," and tyranny is attached to US support for the Arab Muslim tyrants who serve its purposes. Globalization is a major theme in the Arab Muslim media and is almost always raised in connection with US economic penetration. The increasingly miserable economic situation in the Arab Muslim world fuels these frustrations. US dominance, as Arab Muslims see it, indicates where to direct the blame and the resulting hostility (Lewis 2003, 113).

The combination of low productivity with a large and rapidly growing population comprised of many unemployed and uneducated people results in a very frustrated populous. It is this populous that Arab Muslim governments and groups must ensure focuses their attention on external actors rather than internal powers.

Arab Muslims are increasingly aware of the deep and widening gulf between the

opportunities of the free world outside their borders and the appalling privation and

repression within them. The resulting anger is naturally directed first against their rulers

and then against those whom they see as keeping those rulers in power for selfish reasons

(Lewis 2003, 119). Thus, Arab Muslim governments and influential groups must direct

their subjects' attentions and frustrations away from them and onto the US if they want to

remain in power.

What Does It All Mean?

Arab Muslim anti-American sentiment is a very complex issue that can not be

analyzed and explained in simple terms. It is fair to state that there are millions of Arab

Muslims who are indifferent and really have no opinion of the US. However, those who

do have an opinion are likely to be influenced by one or more of the causes investigated

above. That is, what causes anti-American feelings in one person or group may not

necessarily cause it in others. Therefore, the following model to represent the basis and

contributing factors of Arab Muslim anti-American sentiment is proposed.

The large multi-colored oval represents Arab Muslim anti-American sentiment

within an individual or group. The large red arrow at the bottom of the oval represents the

basis of this sentiment which is US regional policies, in particular, US policies in regards

to the Israeli and Palestinian issue. The two smaller, blue arrows at the top represent the

two contributing factors--clash of civilizations and self-interested manipulation by

government or influential Arab Muslim groups--which contribute to the very complex

phenomenon of Arab Muslim anti-Americanism (see figure 6).

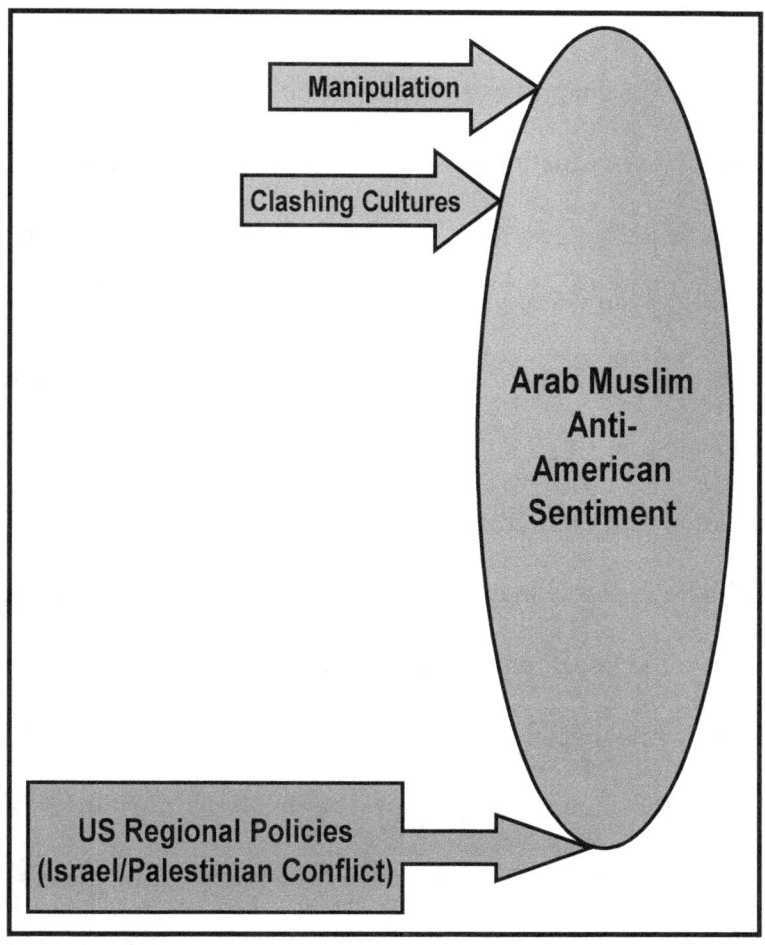

Figure 6.   Arab Muslim Anti-American Model

The oval is multi-colored, but mostly red, because Arab Muslim anti-American

sentiment in individuals and groups is largely based on US regional policies. At the same

time, there is some blue entwined within the oval because both of the smaller blue arrows

contribute to the overall Arab Muslim anti-American sentiment. The oval will likely

change in size and exact color scheme depending upon the particular group or individuals

within the Arab Muslim world, but the basic format and color scheme of the model will

likely not drastically change from one group or person to another.

Summary and Conclusion

The purpose of this chapter was to investigate and analyze the basis and contributing factors of Arab Muslim anti-American sentiment. The recent historical and current statistical evidence suggest that the overall extent of Arab Muslim anti-American sentiment is high throughout the Arab Muslim region. Additionally, the evidence presented confirms that a majority of Arab Muslims attribute these anti-American feelings to US policies in the region, specifically US policies in regards to the Israeli and Palestinian conflict and thus answers the primary research question; Is Arab Muslim antipathy in the Middle East toward the US based on US policies in the region, specifically relating to the Israeli and Palestinian conflict?

Additionally, while investigating the primary research question, this chapter also analyzed other factors that convolute the reason behind Arab Muslim anti-American sentiment. This chapter suggested that there were two contributing factors to this complex phenomenon--clash of civilizations and self-interested manipulation by government or influential Arab Muslim groups--which added to the overall extent and intensity of Arab Muslim anti-American sentiment within the region. Lastly, this chapter suggested that Arab Muslim anti-American sentiment is caused by a combination of US regional policies, clashing cultures and manipulation of information and it is this combination that causes anti-American sentiment to be so high in the region.

Finally, this chapter concluded by suggesting a model that could represent Arab Muslim anti-American sentiment. This model is important because it shows the complexity of this growing phenomenon. The model dissects the causes of the anti-

American phenomenon but also allows people to suggest recommendations suitable to the recognized causes.

The next chapter will further discuss the conclusions of this thesis as well as identify which areas require more research in attempting to determine the basis and factors that cause the overall high extent and intensity of Arab Muslim anti-American sentiment.

CHAPTER 5

CONCLUSIONS AND RECOMMENDATIONS

You [the US] can win the War on Terrorism if you Americans don't forget who you are, if you don't forget who your friends are and if we work together (Friedman 2003, 39).

Jordan's King Abdullah

Introduction

The purpose of this thesis was to investigate and analyze the root causes of anti-American sentiment within the Arab Muslim world. The previous chapters of this thesis investigated the answer to the primary research question: Is Arab Muslim antipathy in the Middle East toward the US based on US policies in the region, specifically relating to the Israeli and Palestinian conflict?

In answering the primary research question, this thesis utilized quantitative survey data to demonstrate the overall degree of anti-American sentiment among Arab Muslims while simultaneously using various other sources to reveal why Arab Muslims possess such negative feelings toward the US. This thesis examined the data to determine if Arab Muslim anti-Americanism is primarily precipitated by America's actions in the region and around the world relating specifically to US policies in support of Israel. Additionally, this thesis investigated and analyzed two additional contributing factors that in conjunction with US polices assisted in determining the overall extent of Arab Muslim anti-American sentiment.

This chapter presents conclusions about the causes of Arab Muslim anti-American sentiment and makes recommendations on how the US could deal with this growing, complex phenomenon. Finally, this chapter will recommend further research that is beyond the scope of this study.

Conclusions

This project illustrated the complexities involved in determining the root causes of Arab Muslim anti-American sentiment. Understanding the various facets of this complex phenomenon is very difficult and thus cannot be explained in simple terms. Thus, to answer the primary research question, this study concludes that Arab Muslim anti-American sentiment is based on US policies in the region, specifically US support for Israel. However, this sentiment is further exemplified due to two other contributing factors--clash of civilizations and self-interested manipulation by Middle Eastern governments or influential Arab groups--which together, increase the overall extent and intensity of Arab Muslim anti-American sentiment within the region.

This thesis showed that Arab Muslim anti-American sentiment currently runs broader and deeper than ever before. Not only is US policy more strongly opposed but the influence of the American lifestyle is now being rejected. Also, for the first time in recent history, American people are now less liked than they were previously. Judging by the trends of the statistics illustrated in this thesis and statistics from other world opinion polls, the negative image of many things American in the Arab Muslim world seems unlikely to change any time soon.

Anti-American sentiment is a pervasive quandary in the Arab Muslim world and is a challenge the US will have to continue to face in the years ahead. Dealing with this growing issue will require the US to distinguish among the differing sources of this sentiment and address each of them appropriately. There will always be some level of anti-American sentiment but by addressing each source independently the US can drastically reduce the overall extent of it. The current, as well as, future challenge is not the complete eradication of Arab Muslim anti-American sentiment but rather its reduction to a level that will allow for normal relations between the US and the Arab world.

Recommendations

Arab Muslim anti-American sentiment is based, not on long-standing hatred of American values, but on more recent anger at US policies in the Middle Eastern region, especially toward Israel. Anti-American sentiment is thus not civilizationally rooted but the growing Arab Muslim civilization and governmental influences do increase the overall extent of it. Therefore, to reduce this anti-American sentiment, the US must understand how its policies directly impact these feelings and aggressively target each of the contributing factors in order to reduce the overall extent of it.

First, the US must launch a serious effort to end the Israeli and Palestinian issue because it is undermining any hope of US and Arab cooperation. The Israeli and Palestinian issue affects everything in the region and nothing will promote greater stability than a more balanced approach toward solving this ongoing conflict. Seriously addressing this issue will go a long way in reducing Arab Muslim anti-American sentiment.

The Israeli and Palestinian issue is very complex and thus will not be easily solved. However, an equitable solution, especially one that leads to recognition of the right of Israel to exist side by side with an independent Palestinian state, will make other problems or issues within the region more manageable.

In fact, a recent world opinion survey showed that a majority of Arab Muslims do believe that if the US was able to broker a peace between Israel and Palestine that their opinion of the US would likely improve (see figure 7).

DUE TO COPYRIGHT RESTRICTIONS,

IMAGES ARE NOT INCLUDED

IN THIS ELECTRONIC EDITION.

Figure 7.   Steps to Improve View of the United States
Source: Anwar Sadat Chair for Peace and Development, University of Maryland/Zogby International, 2006 Annual Arab Public Opinion Survey, A Six Country Study: Egypt, Jordan, Lebanon, Morocco, Saudi Arabia (KSA), and UAE, http://www.bsos.umd.edu/ sadat/2006%20Arab%20Public%20Opinion%20Survey.ppt (accessed on 9 August 2007).

Second, the US should continue to support the spread of democratic values such as justice and fairness in the Arab Muslim world. In conjunction with the spread of these democratic values, the US should support genuine political liberalization and educational and economic reforms. However, the US must accept the outcome and recognize the legitimacy of these democratically elected governments.

Third, the US must be careful about how it utilizes the terms Islam and Islamic terrorism. Irresponsible statements about Islam and the Islamic culture only plays into the hands of radicals who believe the War on Terrorism is essentially a war on Islam and thus increases the division between the Western, Christian culture and Islamic culture.

Fourth, the US needs to make a much bigger investment in public diplomacy in the Muslim world and vigorously challenge what is published there. The US should show a higher degree of respect for its allies in the region and counter publish anti-American claims of genocide, murder, or oppression.

Lastly, the US must force its allies within the Arab region to shoulder some of this responsibility. That is, the US needs political and religious Arab leaders to provide an ideological alternative to the politics and resentment peddled by radicals. The US must force these leaders to promote and allow public dissent and not to deflect this dissent away from them and onto the US.

Recommended Further Research

This research was conducted to answer one specific question. However, there are other ways to investigate and analyze the causes of Arab Muslim anti-American sentiment, and in order to truly understand it one must constantly review the potential causes of this phenomenon.

One of the aims of this study was not only to show the current extent of Arab Muslim anti-Americanism and identify its basis and contributing factors but also to initiate further discussion about the topic. To improve on this study it would help to analyze other specific US policies in the region and the wars in Iraq and Afghanistan to see how they contribute to Arab Muslim anti-American sentiment.

79

REFERENCE LIST

Anwar Sadat Chair for Peace and Development. 2004. Arab attitudes toward political and social issues, foreign policy and the media. A public opinion poll conducted jointly by the Anwar Sadat Chair for Peace and Development at the University of Maryland and Zogby International. May. http://www.bsos.umd.edu/sadat/pub/Arab%20Attitudes%20Towards%20Political%20and%20Social%20Issues,%20Foreign%20Policy%20and%20the%20Media.htm (accessed 18 June 2007).

Anwar Sadat Chair for Peace and Development, University of Maryland/Zogby International. 2006. Annual Arab public opinion survey. A six country study: Egypt, Jordan, Lebanon, Morocco, Saudi Arabia (KSA), and UAE. http://www.bsos.umd.edu/sadat/2006%20Arab%20Public%20Opinion%20Survey.ppt (accessed 9 August 2007).

Barr, Cameron W. 2001. Young, educated and anti-American. *Christian Science Monitor* 93, no. 213:6. Combined Arms Research Library, EBSCOhost, Academic Search Complete. http://web.ebscohost.com/ehost/detail?vid=27&hid=115&sid=3489c4d4-3622-4879-8147-042816148ded%40sessionmgr104 (accessed 28 February 2007).

Battah, Abdalla M. 2006. Proximate and permissive causes of anti-Americanism in the Arab Middle East. Minnesota State University, Mankato. EBSCOhost Academic Search Premier. http://search.ebscohost.com (accessed 30 March 2007).

Breyfogle, Todd. 2004. The spiritual roots of anti-Americanism. *Reviews in Religion & Theology* 11, no. 2:257-262. Combined Arms Research Library, EBSCOhost, Academic Search Complete. http://web.ebscohost.com/ehost/pdf?vid=23&hid=115&sid=3489c4d4-3622-4879-8147-042816148ded%40sessionmgr104 (accessed 30 March 2007).

Business Week. 2003. America: The view from abroad. *Business Week*, no. 3837 (16 June): 104. Combined Arms Research Library, EBSCOhost, Academic Search Complete. http://web.ebscohost.com/ehost/detail?vid=33&hid=103&sid=e092b188-6c8c-4770-b095-dd707fac6dfd%40sessionmgr102 (accessed 28 February 2007).

Chiozza, Giacomo. 2005. Love and hate: Anti-Americanism and the American world order. Conference Papers--Southern Political Science Association: 1-47. Annual Meeting, New Orleans, LA. Combined Arms Research Library, EBSCOhost, Academic Search Complete. http://search.ebscohost.com/login.aspx?direct=true&db=a9h&AN=18604137&site=ehost-live (accessed 30 March 2007).

CNN.com. 2006. Hamas' past cast shadow over peace plans. http://www.cnn.com/2006/WORLD/meast/01/26/palestinian.election/index.html (accessed 5 August 2007).

Cole, Juan. 2006. AHR forum: Anti-Americanism: It's the policies. *The American Historical Review* 111, no. 4 (October): 1120-1129. http://www.history cooperative.org/journals/ahr/111.4/cole.html (accessed 25 March 2007).

Crockett, Richard. 2004. No common ground? Islam, anti-Americanism and the United States[1]. *European Journal of American Culture* 23, no. 2:125-142. Combined Arms Research Library, EBSCOhost, Academic Search Complete. http://web. ebscohost.com/ehost/pdf?vid=14&hid=104&sid=6667bdd4-4fa2-4da3-adb0-0bac11ecf637%40sessionmgr103 (accessed 30 March 2007).

D'Souza, Dinesh. 2007. *The enemy at home: The cultural left and its responsibility for 9/11.* New York: Doubleday Books.

Darley, William M. COL, USA. 2007. The necessity for values operations as opposed to information operations in Iraq and Afghanistan. *Air and Space Power Journal* 21, no. 1 (Spring). http://www.airpower.maxwell.af.mil/airchronicles/apj/apj07/ spr07/darleyspr07.html (accessed 2 July 2007).

Economist. 2004. They grumble, but they move. *Economist* 370, no. 8365:41. Combined Arms Research Library, EBSCOhost, Academic Search Complete. http://web. ebscohost.com/ehost/detail?vid=36&hid=103&sid=e092b188-6c8c-4770-b095-dd707fac6dfd%40sessionmgr102 (accessed 28 February 2007).

------. 2005. The view from abroad. *Economist* 374, no. 8414:24-26. Combined Arms Research Library, EBSCOhost, Academic Search Complete. http://web. ebscohost.com/ehost/detail?vid=8&hid=104&sid=6667bdd4-4fa2-4da3-adb0-0bac11ecf637%40sessionmgr103 (accessed 28 February 2007).

Esposito, John L. 2006. It's the policy, stupid: Political Islam and U.S. foreign policy, *The Harvard International Review* (2 November). http://www.csmonitor.com/ 2007/0222/p99s01-duts.html (accessed 13 March 2007).

Fouad, Ajami. 2001. The sentry's solitude. *Foreign Affairs* (November/December). http://www.foreignpolicy.com/story/cms.php?story_id=29 (accessed 10 April 2007).

Friedman, Thomas L. 2003. *Longitudes and attitudes: The world in the age of terrorism.* New York: Anchor Books.

Gallup World Poll. 2006. *Special report: Muslim world.* Princeton, NJ: The Gallup Organization. http://media.gallup.com/WorldPoll/PDF/GALLUP+MUSLIM+ STUDIES_Moderate+v+Extremist+Views_11.13.06_FINAL.pdf (accessed 2 July 2007).

Gardels, Nathan. 2003. The future of anti-Americanism. *NPQ: New Perspectives Quarterly* 20, no. 2 (Spring): 2. Combined Arms Research Library, EBSCOhost,

Academic Search Premier. http://search.ebscohost.com/login.aspx?direct=
true&db=a9h&AN=9871180&site=ehost-live (accessed 30 March 2007).

Gilgoff, Dan, and Jay Tolson. 2003. Losing friends? *U.S. News & World Report* 134, no.
8:40. Combined Arms Research Library, EBSCOhost, Academic Search Premier.
http://search.ebscohost.com/login.aspx?direct=true&db=a9h&AN=9263561&site
=ehost-live (accessed 5 March 2007).

Global Scan Archives. n.d. Global poll finds religion and culture are not to blame for
tensions between Islam and the West. *BBC World Service Poll.* http://www.
globescan.com/news_archives/bbciswest/detail.html (accessed 18 June 2007).

Habeck, Mary. 2006. *Knowing the enemy: Jihadist ideology and the war on terror.* New
Haven: Yale University Press.

Hilsum, Lindsey. 2005. World view. *New Statesman* 134, no. 4732:8-8. Combined Arms
Research Library, EBSCOhost, Academic Search Premier. http://search.ebsco
host.com/login.aspx?direct=true&db=a9h&AN=18014976&site=ehost-live
(accessed 28 February 2007).

Hollander, Paul. 2002. The politics of envy. *New Criterion* 21, no. 3:14-19. Combined
Arms Research Library, EBSCOhost, Academic Search Premier. http://search.
ebscohost.com/login.aspx?direct=true&db=a9h&AN=7719387&site=ehost-live
(accessed 30 March 2007).

Huntington, Samuel P. 1996. *The clash of civilizations and the remaking of world order.*
New York: Simon and Schuster.

Kohut, Andrew, and Bruce Stokes. 2006. *America against the world.* New York: Time
Books.

La Guardia, Anton. 2003. *War without end: Israelis, Palestinians, and the struggle for a
promise land.* New York: Thomas Dunne Books.

Leffler, Melvyn P. 2004. Bush's foreign policy. *Foreign Policy* no. 144: 22-28.
Combined Arms Research Library, EBSCOhost, Academic Search Premier.
http://web.ebscohost.com/ehost/detail? vid=7&hid=115&sid=0ac50e50-bef4-
42fc-8ca2-5e6df9761535%40 sessionmgr107 (accessed 5 March 2007).

Lewis, Bernard. 2003. *The crisis of Islam: Holy war and unholy terror.* New York:
Random House.

Linzer, Dafna. 2004. Poll shows growing Arab rancor at U.S. *Washington Post* (23 July).
http://www.washingtonpost.com/wp-dyn/articles/A7080-2004Jul22.html
(accessed 25 March 2007).

Makdisi, Ussama. 2002. Anti-Americanism in the Arab world: An interpretation of a brief history. *Journal of American History* 89, no. 2:538-557. Combined Arms Research Library, EBSCOhost, Academic Search Premier. http://search.ebsco host.com/login.aspx?direct=true&db=a9h&AN=7390237&site=ehost-live (accessed 30 March 2007).

Masland, Tom, Christopher Dickey, Ron Moreau, Dan Ephron, Adrian McIntyre, and Gameela Ismail. 2003. The rage next time. *Newsweek* 141, no. 15:49. Combined Arms Research Library, EBSCOhost, Academic Search Premier. http://web. ebscohost.com/ehost/ detail?vid=17&hid=115&sid=0ac50e50-bef4-42fc-8ca2-5e6df9761535%40 sessionmgr107 (accessed 28 February 2007).

Mendieta, Eduardo. 2003. Patriotism and anti-Americanism. *Peace Review* 15, no. 4:435-442. Combined Arms Research Library, EBSCOhost, Academic Search Premier. http://web.ebscohost.com/ehost/ pdf?vid=18&hid=115&sid=0ac50e50-bef4-42fc-8ca2-5e6df9761535%40 sessionmgr107 (accessed 30 March 2007).

Mogahed, Dalia, and Genieve Abdo. 2006. Muslims and Americans: The way forward. *Gallup World Poll*. http://media.gallup.com/WorldPoll/PDF/GALLUP+ MUSLIM+STUDIES_Islam+and+West_2.1.07_FINAL.pdf (accessed 5 March 2007).

Naim, Moises. 2003. The perils of lite anti-Americanism. *Foreign Policy* (May/June). http://www.foreignpolicy.com/story/cms.php?story_id=29 (accessed 10 April 2007).

The Nation. 2005. Unintended consequences: A forum on Iraq and the Mideast. *The Nation* (15 August): 20-25. http://www.thenation.com/doc/20050815/forum (accessed on 5 March 2007).

Nevo Joseph, and Ilan Pappe, eds. 1994. *Jordan in Asad's greater Syria strategy, Jordan in the middle east, 1948-1988: The making of pivotal state*. http://www.amazon. com/gp/reader/0714634549/ref=sib_dp_pt/102-5730769-9095365#reader-link (accessed on 7 October 2007).

Ohlund, Barbara, and Chong-ho Yu. 1999. *Threats to validity of research design*. http://www.creative-wisdom.com/teaching/WBI/threat.shtml (accessed 1 July 2007).

Parapan, Manuela. 2005. Why Arabs are anti-U.S. *World & I* 20, no. 1. Combined Arms Research Library, EBSCOhost, MasterFILE Premier. http://search.ebscohost. com/login.aspx?direct=true&db=f5h&AN=16264852&site=ehost-live (accessed 29 March 2007).

Pew Research Center. 2004. A year after Iraq war: Mistrust of America in Europe ever higher, Muslim anger persists. *Pew Global Project Attitudes* (16 March).

http://people-press.org/reports/display.php3? ReportID=206 (accessed 13 March and 2 July 2007).

------. 2005a. America's character gets mixed reviews: US image up slightly but still negative (23 June). http://pewglobal.org/reports/display.php? ReportID=247 (accessed 2 July 2007).

------. 2005b. Islamic extremism: Common concern for Muslim and western publics; Support for terror wanes among Muslim publics. *Pew Global Project Attitudes* (14 July). http://pewglobal.org/reports/display.php?Report ID=248 (accessed 13 March 2007).

------. 2007. *Rising environmental concern in 47-nation survey: Global unease with major world powers.* Washington, DC: Pew Research Center, 27 June. http://pewglobal.org/reports/display.php?ReportID=256 (accessed 2 July 2007).

Power, Carla, and Christopher Dickey. 2002. Muhammad Atta's neighborhood. *Newsweek* 140, no. 25:36. Combined Arms Research Library, EBSCOhost, Academic Search Premier. http://search.ebscohost.com/login.aspx?direct= true&db=a9h&AN=8637539&site=ehost-live (accessed 5 March 2007).

Regan, Tom. 2007. Polls show anti-American feelings at all time high in Muslim countries. *Christian Science Monitor*, 22 February http://www.csmonitor.com/ 2007/ 0222/p99s01-duts.html (accessed 19 March 2007).

Rubin, Barry. 2002. The reel roots of Arab anti-Americanism. *Foreign Affairs* 81, no. 6:73-85. Combined Arms Research Library, EBSCOhost, Academic Search Premier. http://search.ebscohost.com/login.aspx?direct=true&db=a9h&AN= 7568963&site=ehost-live (accessed 30 March 2007).

Rubin, Barry, and Judith Colp Rubin. 2004. Anti-Americanism re-examined. *Brown Journal of World Affairs* 11, no. 1:17-24. Combined Arms Research Library, EBSCOhost. Academic Search Premier. http://web.ebscohost.com/ehost/pdf?vid= 54&hid=115&sid=0ac50e50-bef4-42fc-8ca2-5e6df9761535%40sessionmgr107 (accessed 30 March 2007).

Sardar, Ziauddin, and Merryl Wyn Davies. 2004. *Why do people hate America.* Cambridge: Icon Books.

Sharansky, Natan, and Ron Dermer. 2004. *The case for democracy: The power of freedom to overcome tyranny and terror.* New York: Public Affairs.

Syed, Aijaz Zaka. 2007. Here is why they love and hate US. *Khaleej Times Online* (3 March). http://www.khaleejtimes.com/DisplayArticleNew.asp?xfile=data/ opinion/2007/March/opinion_March11.xml&section=opinion&col (accessed 13 March 2007).

Vedrine, Hubert. 2004. On anti-Americanism. *Brown Journal of World Affairs* 10, no. 2:117-121. Combined Arms Research Library, EBSCOhost. Academic Search Premier. http://web.ebscohost.com/ ehost/pdf?vid=60&hid=115&sid=0ac50e50-bef4-42fc-8ca2-5e6df9761535% 40sessionmgr107 (accessed 30 March 2007).

World Press Reiew. 2001. Dishonest broker. *World Press Review* 48, no. 8 (August). http://www.worldpress.org/0801cover5.htm (accessed 18 June 2007).

WorldPublicOpinion.Org. 2007a. Global views of the US: Middle East backgrounder, 22 January. http://www.worldpublicopinion.org/pipa/pdf/jan07/BBC_USRole_ Jan07_bgmideast.pdf (accessed 18 June 2007).

--------. 2007b. Global views on relations between Islam and the West: Middle East backgrounder, 22 January. http://www.worldpublicopinion.org/pipa/pdf/ jan07/BBC_USRole_Jan07_bgmideast.pdf (accessed 18 June 2007).

Zogby International. 2006. Five nation survey of the Middle East, Submitted to: Arab American Institute. December. http://aai.3cdn.net/96d8eeaec55ef4c217_ m9m6b97wo.pdf (accessed 2 July 2007).

Zunes, Stephen. 2001. 10 things to know about U.S. policy in the Middle East. 26 September. http://www.alternet.org/story/11592/ (accessed 20 March 2007).